BLUE COLLAR CHAMPIONS

BY JOHN HAREAS

PHOTOGRAPHY BY NBA ENTERTAINMENT PHOTOS

THE OFFICIAL
NBA FINALS 2004
RETROSPECTIVE

PUBLISHED BY CANUM ENTERTAINMENT & NBA ENTERTAINMENT

CANUM

ACKNOWLEDGEMENTS

Total Team Effort .... Similar to the Pistons' inspired championship run, *Blue Collar Champions* demonstrated a selfless display of hard work and commitment among a group of dedicated professionals who deserve special praise .... *All day you've been working that hard line* .... The coach, the architect and visionary of this finely-tuned high-octane machine, Charlie Rosenzweig, who made sure we worked and executed the right way .... *Coming home at the end of the working day* ... Joe Amati and Scott Yurdin shattering photo essay records while raising the standard of photo editing, meticulously incorporating the very best high-energy and all-access sports photography around ..... *Loud let the bells them ring ... For here they come with banners flying ... Far we their praises tell* ... Michael Levine, the Ann Arbor legend, who brilliantly meshed the creative and marketing across all platforms so that all of the colors seamlessly bled into one .... *And the wizards play down on Pinball Way on the boardwalk way past dark* .... Matthew Krautheim and Paul Ward, the men who tirelessly laid it all on the line every day, proofing and fact-checking and Mario Argote and David Mintz who always deliver...... *I got a sixty-nine Chevy with a 396 Fuelie heads and a Hurst on the floor* ... David Bonilla, Bennett Renda, John Kristofick overseeing and executing the sheer volume of high-res photography ..... *Now if you're lookin' for a hero* .... Nat Butler, Andy Bernstein, Jesse Garrabrant, Allen Einstein and the rest of the NBA photographers — thank you.... *When you need me just call my name* ...Thank you to everyone at Razorfish, particularly Jim Forni, Steve Polacek and the ultimate sixth man designer, Mark Alper, who set the tone in creating this beautifully designed book .... *Champions of the world* ... Joe Dumars, Matt Dobek and Kevin Grigg for providing us with unprecedented access and assistance throughout the season ... *'Cause I got me a promise I ain't afraid to make* ... To Jennifer, Emma and Christopher who continue to overwhelm me with their love and support — John Hareas, July 2004

PHOTOGRAPHY CREDITS

NBAE Photographers **Allen Einstein:** BackCover, 8, 9, 10, 11, 18, 19, 20, 21, 22, 23, 24, 25, 26, 27, 28, 29, 30, 32, 33, 34, 35, 36, 37, 38, 39, 40, 41, 42, 43, 44, 45, 46, 47, 48, 49, 51, 56, 57, 58, 59, 70, 71, 81, 90, 97, 98, 100, 101, 108, 109, 110, 111 **Andrew D. Bernstein:** Front Cover, Back Cover, 1, 7, 13, 17, 27, 35, 49, 50, 60, 61, 62, 63, 64, 65, 66, 67, 68, 69, 72, 73, 74, 75, 76, 77, 79, 81, 82, 83, 84, 85, 86, 87.88, 89, 90, 91, 92, 93, 94, 97, 99, 101, 103, 105, 106, 107, 108, 109, 110, 111 **Nathaniel S. Butler:** 10, 11, 15, 16, 18, 32, 33, 36, 37, 38, 43, 49, 58, 62, 63, 64, 66, 68, 69, 71, 73, 74, 75, 77, 78, 80, 82, 84, 85, 86, 87, 89, 91, 92, 93, 94, 95, 97, 100, 102, 103, 104, 105, 106, 110, 111, 112 **Jesse D. Garrabrant:** Back Cover, 19, 28, 40, 41, 44, 47, 48, 49, 54, 56, 57, 59, 66, 67, 68, 69, 70, 71, 75, 76, 77, 81, 89, 90, 91, 92, 93, 100, 101, 104, 105, 106, 107, 108, 110, **Gregory Shamus:** Back Cover, 9, 11, 20, 21, 23, 34, 39, 41, 42, 43, 45, 46, 71, 80, 81 **David Sherman:** 32, 70, 100 **Catherine Steenkeste:** 71, 80, 81 **Garrett W. Ellwood:** 39, 76, 77, 78, 101, 102, 103, 107, 108, 111 **Jennifer Pottheiser:** 46, 52, 53, 63, 82 **Terrence Vaccaro:** 56, 62, 77, 84, 87 **Noah Graham:** 46 **Andy Hayt:** 33, 62, 66, 67 **Kent Horner:** 2, 3, 69, 76, 77 **Scott Quintard:** 80, 81 **Robert Sario:** 80 **Chris Ivey:** 80 **Ron Hoskins:** 34, 37, 38, 58 **Ron Turenne:** 29, 33, 42, 43, 46 **Sam Forencich:** 32, 37, 41, 42 **Gary Dineen:** 32, 39, 54, 55 **Fernando Medina:** 38, 40, 42, 43, 45 **Victor Baldizon:** 43, 45 **Tom Pidgeon:** 49 **Jeff Reinking:** 50 **Barry Gossage:** 43 **Noren Trotman:** 33, 37, 41, 48 **Tim Defrisco:** 33 **Scott Cunningham:** 16, 42 **NBA Photos:** 12, 14, 15, 17, 18, 27 **Naismith Memorial Basketball Hall of Fame:** 14 **Rocky Widner:** 12, 27, 38, 45 **Lou Capozzola:** 17 **D. Clarke Evans:** 18, 35, 36 **Dale Tait:** 18 **Bill Baptist:** 19, 35, 36 **Ray Amati:** 28, 41 *Getty Photographers* **Jed Jacobsohn:** Back Cover, 45, 80, 92, 101, 103, 108 **Stephen Dunn:** 63, 75 **Jonathan Daniel:** 12, 18, 40, 48, 54 **Elsa:** 86, 89, 101, 102, 104, 110 **Andy Lyons:** 44

SPECIAL THANKS

AT NBAE PHOTOS: Joe Amati, David Bonilla, Scott Yurdin, Brian Choi, Pam Costello, John Kristofick, Bennet Renda **AT NBAE:** Adam Silver, Gregg Winik, Charles Rosenzweig, Paul Hirschheimer, Ken Adelson, Marc Hirschheimer, Michael Levine, Mario Argote, David Mintz, Tony Stewart, Rob Sario, Matt Krautheim, Paul Ward **AT THE PISTONS:** Bill Davidson, Tom Wilson, Joe Dumars, Larry Brown, Dan Hauser, John Ciszewski, Peter Skorich, Matt Dobek, Craig Turnbull, Kevin Grigg and the entire Pistons organization **AT THE NBA:** David Stern, Russ Granik, Tim Andree, Brian McIntyre, Terry Lyons, Tim Frank **AT RAZORFISH:** Mark Alper, Jim Forni, Liz Jarvis, Nick Lo Bue, Carol Monk, Iris Brenk, Steve Polacek **AT CANUM ENTERTAINMENT:** John Moores Jr., Jennifer Moores, Rob Zeps, Amy Campbell **AT PROFESSIONAL GRAPHICS:** David Goley, Jane Messenger **AT SOMERSET GRAPHICS:** Doug Thomson, Ian Budge, Jeff Krotser

2003-2004 NBA CHAMPIONS DVD

Continue to relive the excitement of The Finals with the Official 2003-2004 NBA Champions DVD, featuring exclusive behind-the-scenes footage and interviews. From the season opener to the Game 5 Finals clincher, this special edition DVD highlights one of the greatest seasons in Detroit Pistons history. Available wherever videos are sold.

CANUM

PUBLISHED BY:
Canum Entertainment LLC, 977A Lomas Santa Fe Drive, Solana Beach, CA 92075
NBA Entertainment, 450 Harmon Meadow Blvd. Secaucus, NJ 07094

razorfish

DESIGNED AND PRODUCED BY:
Razorfish, 600 W Fulton Street #400, Chicago, Illinois 60661

PRINTED BY:
Somerset Graphics Co, Ltd, 370 Brunel Road, Mississauga, Ontario, Canada L4Z 2C2

ISBN 1-932938-02-8
Printed in Canada
9 8 7 6 5 3 2
[FIRST EDITION]

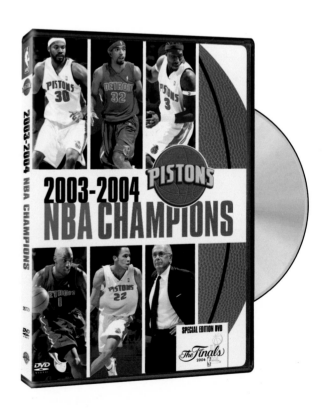

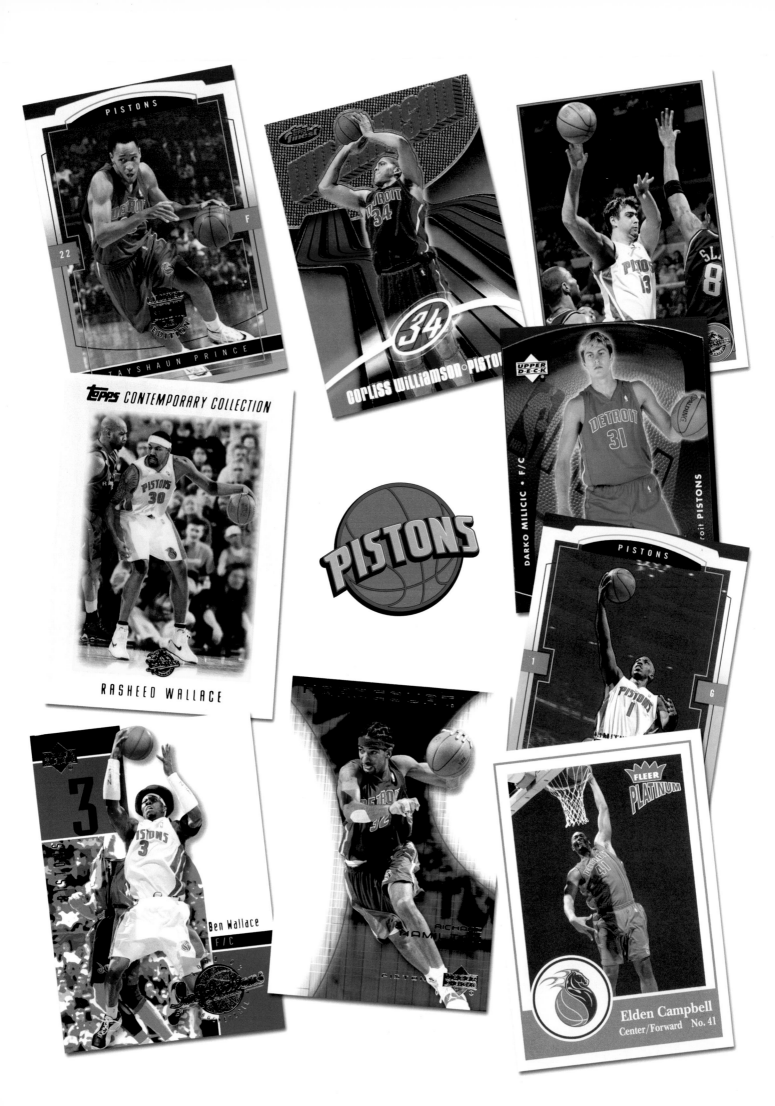

CONTENTS

Hard Work
Pays Off

TOTAL TEAM EFFORT

BY JOE DUMARS

The tone for this past season was set one week after the conclusion of our 2002-03 season. We had just been swept in the Eastern Conference Finals by the New Jersey Nets and seven days later, we had a new coach on board. The move was sudden, drastic and really caught a lot of people by surprise. Our former coach, Rick Carlisle, did a great job for us for two seasons. The team showed significant improvement, reaching the second round of the playoffs in his first season and the following year, advancing even further. Despite this progress, I still felt like something was missing to reach the next level. We had a nucleus of young, hungry and aggressive players that needed someone to bring a sense of urgency, a sense of passion, and to be a driving force who would keep them on their toes all season long. We needed a championship difference. We needed Larry Brown.

The move to bring one of the game's premier teachers and a Hall of Fame coach sent a clear message to all of our fans, players, media and really everyone in the organization that we were serious about becoming NBA champions — this season. A lot was written about the move and why it was done and a lot of the experts openly questioned it. But one has to understand that when you sit atop of an organization, you know what's best for your players, even if it's not apparent from the outside looking in. Once Larry became available, I didn't think twice about it. I knew he was our man.

During training camp in October, it was apparent that there was a new sense of urgency amongst the players. You saw it in their practice habits and you saw it in the preseason games. There was understandably going to be a transition process with a new coach on board and it would take some time to incorporate a new philosophy. The team experienced some early struggles, compiling a 14-10 record by mid-December. I thought the players were trying to do too much. They weren't fighting what Larry was saying, if anything, they were too intent on doing exactly what he was instructing. It looked like they stopped playing naturally, lacking the necessary flow. As time went on, they realized what Larry wanted, and they could incorporate the strengths of their games and his directives at the same time. That's when I really thought we took off as a team and it started to reflect in the standings. The team reeled off 13 straight wins from the end of December all the way through January 19. As they were finding their footing and identity under Larry, we still felt we were a player away from putting us over the top.

In late February, we acquired what turned out to be the final piece of our championship puzzle — Rasheed Wallace. This move did several things for us. It gave us tremendous salary cap flexibility; we ended up moving a couple of guys who had a few years left on their contracts for a one-year player. Secondly, it gave us a superstar talent

who could help us immediately in Rasheed. In terms of frontcourt players in the NBA, he ranks among the elite. Even though he doesn't post 20 and 10 numbers anymore, he's that type of talent.

We also acquired someone that I felt this team desperately needed – a player with an edge. Rasheed brings a certain streak to him that you just can't find in a lot of players. We needed someone who would bring some fire and a certain nastiness onto the court. He brought all of those things and more, and they became infectious. His personality became contagious on the floor, in the locker room and on the team bus. He changed the complexion of who we were.

I was confident that Rasheed would make an easy transition to our environment, which I feel is the best in the NBA. We have good men here. From the coaching staff, to the scouts, to the players, we have no out-of-control egos where the focus is, "It's all about me." I knew Rasheed was an unselfish person who was a complete

end of the game just to get over the 70-point threshold, which they did, reaching 71, and bringing an end to this historic streak. However, the winning streak continued in impressive fashion to the tune of eight straight games. It was at that point in the season when I was convinced that this team could win the NBA championship.

As the playoffs approached, we wanted to get off to a strong start. We knew we had to be physical and take control of our first-round opponent, the Milwaukee Bucks. They like to run up and down and we didn't want them to get out in the open court and run wild. We had to impose our will on them early in the series and we did, winning in five games.

The Eastern Conference Semifinals featured our nemesis, the Nets, a team that provided us with a long summer. Any changes we made during the offseason were a direct reflection of how we lost in that series. We knew this was going to be a huge test for us. I felt, mentally, we were ready for this series as well as any

team player and that in these surroundings, he would come in and fit in without any problems whatsoever.

Within two weeks of Rasheed coming aboard, our defense, which had been good up to that point, really elevated to another level. We set an NBA record by holding opponents under 70 points for five consecutive games. Road contests in Portland, Denver, Seattle and home games versus Chicago and Philadelphia displayed this team's tenacious defense. That streak galvanized this team as much as anything we accomplished during the regular season. Even though we had a 13-game winning streak earlier, which was a boon to our overall record, the defensive stretch served as a strong indicator to the players that they could accomplish something special. This is very important, especially if you've never won a championship before.

Besides, the team knew they must be good when an opponent such as the Nets intentionally fouled at the

series that we had played. We jumped out to a 2-0 lead only to watch them come back to win the next three. Since they were the two-time Eastern Conference Champions, we knew they had a lot of pride and that this series was going to be a real dogfight. The remaining two games came down to who had the will to do whatever it took to win. When we defeated the Nets in seven games, I thought that we were prepared to beat anybody in the NBA, East or West.

In the next round, I thought the Indiana Pacers matched up with us as well as anyone in the league. They're deep, have pretty good size and I knew Rick would have them prepared. I thought that it was going to be a tough matchup, but I believed that our experience would win out – and it played out that way.

After advancing to the NBA Finals, it appeared the series was over before it even started. No one gave a team that won 54 regular-season games and split the season series against the Los Angeles Lakers, a team featuring four-future Hall of Famers, any chance to win. The question on everyone's mind was whether the series would be over in four or five games.

Prior to Game 1, our confidence was sky high. We all looked at each other and said, "We're better than the Lakers. We're deeper, we're stronger, we're bigger." We didn't see how they could beat us. Our thinking was, "Shaq and Kobe could both get 30, and that's not going to beat us. Sixty points is not going to stop us from realizing our goal." There wasn't any one in the organization who didn't believe we couldn't defeat the Lakers.

Winning Game 1, 87-75, was a great start for us, but even after giving them the second game, I wasn't concerned going into Game 3. We had experienced a heartbreaking loss in triple overtime at home in Game 5 against the Nets three weeks earlier in the Eastern Conference Semifinals. Two days later, we walked into

we were up 3-1, some people still weren't convinced. Once again it seemed like they were watching a different series.

I had been hesitant to make any type of comparisons with this current team to the 1989 and 1990 championship Pistons teams on which I played. But now that this team has won a title, I can finally exhale and say that there are a few similarities that could be drawn. Both teams were exceptional on defense, tremendously deep, both depended on a balanced attack and were all about displaying a complete team effort.

What is better: winning as a player or as an executive? Both are certainly sweet. As a player, it always seemed more exciting to win a title. But in my current position, as President of Basketball Operations, when you have to build a team from scratch and then are able to watch it grow into an NBA champion, it is that much more gratifying for me personally — especially in front of these loyal fans.

I'm so happy that my players received the chance to ride in the championship parade and had the opportunity

Jersey and won on their own court, and eventually closed them out in seven games. We had been up 2-1 against Indiana, and could have been up 3-1, but lost to them and gave them back home-court advantage, and still we went back there and won. So, when we lost Game 2 in L.A., and people asked, "How is this going to affect the Detroit Pistons' psyche?" I was wondering if any of these people raising the question had ever watched us play, because we had proven time and time again that, mentally, no one is going to be stronger than us. Plus, we were about to play three consecutive games in Detroit.

Some people may characterize this Finals as an upset, but upsets occur in the NCAA Tournament, where one game is all that matters. You don't get upsets in four or five straight games or in seven-game series. It simply means that the winning team is the better team. We felt like we were the better team the entire series. Even when

to see a million absolutely fanatical people in downtown Detroit screaming for two straight hours, and then return to The Palace and find even more waiting to celebrate. The players walked up to me after it was over and said they had no idea that people could be this passionate. It was great for the players to see this kind of response to everything they had accomplished. Now they understand, even more so, what they mean to this city. Their commitment to the game, to each other and the hard work that they put in to win the title struck a chord with the fans of this city.

Like Larry always likes to say, "Play the right way" and these guys did. What more can you ask? ◯

[signature]

HISTORY

It is a franchise of distinction, one that pre-dated the NBA and one that produced some of the game's greatest players: McDermott, Jeannette, Yardley, DeBusschere, Bing, Lanier, Thomas and Dumars. It possessed a visionary owner, Fred Zollner, whose leadership and financial resources helped keep a newly expanded league afloat, one that nearly 60 years later enjoys unprecedented global

Bobby McDermott, a tough 5-11 guard who owned the best two-handed set shot of his era and would later be voted the greatest Zollner Piston of all time. McDermott along with the era's other premier backcourt player, Buddy Jeannette, had the Pistons firing on all cylinders, as Fort Wayne boasted the league's best record from 1943 through 1946, winning back-to-back NBL titles in '44 and '45.

> ## "In those days, you would drive into town and look for the biggest building. We drove up to this bar and I got out of the car and ran inside and I said to the bartender, 'Hey, we are supposed to play a basketball game in this town today, can you tell me where it is?' He said, 'This is the place.'"
>
> BUDDY JEANNETTE, FORT WAYNE PISTONS

popularity. Its current owner, William Davidson, is one of the most respected and innovative businessmen in all of professional sports.

The Pistons' history is rich with great memories, moments and tradition. The origins of the franchise can be traced 190 miles south of Detroit to Fort Wayne, Ind., the hometown of Zollner's piston manufacturing company, Zollner Machine Works. The team was founded in 1941 as the Zollner Pistons and competed in the National Basketball League (NBL), which began as the Midwest Basketball Conference in 1935 and changed its name in 1937 with hopes of attracting a larger fan base. It was a league that was ahead of its time when it came to the marriage of professional sports and corporate commercialization, boasting such team names as the Akron Firestone Non-Skids, the Akron Goodyear Wingfoots and the Toledo Jim White Chevrolets. Thanks to Zollner, the Pistons traveled in style, criss-crossing the Midwest in their own team plane, a DC-3.

Fort Wayne posted a 15-9 record in its inaugural season and reached the NBL Finals before losing to the Oshkosh All-Stars, a powerhouse which appeared in the championship series five consecutive times (1938-42), winning two titles. The Pistons featured perennial league MVP

The Pistons may have traveled by air but when it came to venues, the accommodations weren't so convenient. It wasn't uncommon for the Pistons to play their games in armories, ballrooms, high school gyms or even taverns.

"In those days, you would drive into town and look for the biggest building," recalled Jeannette. "We drove up to this bar and I got out of the car and ran inside and I said to the bartender, 'Hey, we are supposed to play a basketball game in this town today, can you tell me where it is?' He said, 'This is the place.' I looked around and there were tables all over the place. After we got dressed they had shoved all the tables back and put a basket on one wall, and on the other side they had a basket drawn up into the ceiling. The referee drew a big circle on the middle of the floor, and a net dropped down around the floor. And the damnedest fight you ever saw started. That was a real education."

In 1948, the Pistons, along with three other teams from the NBL, joined the Basketball Association of America (BAA), which absorbed the remains of the 13-year-old league after the season. It was a merger which Zollner played a pivotal role in overseeing. The BAA then adopted a new name prior to the 1949-50 season, the National Basketball Association. Due to the popularity of the college

Fort Wayne Whips Celtics in Opener

FORT WAYNE, Ind., Nov. 2 (AP)—The Fort Wayne Pistons cut loose with their fast break in the second half and won a 107-84 victory over the Boston Celtics tonight.

Fort Wayne held only a 47-45 lead at the half. It was the opening game of the National Basket Ball Association for each team.

FORT WAYNE (107)	G	F	TP	BOSTON (84)	G	F	TP
Schaus f....	3	8	14	Walker f....	0	0	0
Riffey f....	4	0	8	Cooper f....	3	1	7
Hargis f....	2	2	6	Leede f....	2	4	8
Burris f....	3	0	6	Stanczak f..	1	7	9
Foust c....	8	5	21	Duncan f...	2	3	7
Kerris,c-f..	3	6	12	Macauley c.	3	3	9
Johnson g..	5	2	12	Mahnken c.	3	0	6
Carpenter g.	0	2	2	Herzberg g.	1	4	6
Oldham g..	5	1	11	Cousy g....	4	8	16
Klueh g....	5	5	15	Donham g...	4	1	9
				Sailors g....	2	3	7
Totals ..38	31	107		Totals 25	34	84	

1941-48	1949-57	1957	1957-58	1959

Automobile-piston magnate Fred Zollner launches the club in 1941 in Fort Wayne, Indiana, christening it the Fort Wayne Zollner Pistons. The Pistons join the National Basketball League (NBL), which consists primarily of teams fielded by Midwest corporations. In the early years, the team plays home games at Fort Wayne's North Side High School. The team wins two National Basketball League championships during World War II (1944 and 1945), when many players are not drafted into the military because they work in the owner's plant, helping make pistons for military aircraft and machinery.

Following the 1949 playoffs the NBL and Basketball Association of America (BAA) merge to form the National Basketball Association. The Pistons are placed in the Central Division, the league's toughest, along with the Minneapolis Lakers and the Rochester Royals. The team reaches the NBA Finals in consecutive seasons, falling to both the Syracuse Nationals (in seven games in 1955) and Philadelphia Warriors (in five games in 1956). Between 1952 and 1957, Fort Wayne plays its home games at the Allen County War Memorial Coliseum. The Pistons win the Western Division regular season crown in each of the 1954-55, '55-56 (outright) and '56-57 (tied three-way) seasons.

Franchise moves to Detroit but keeps the Pistons nickname, which still seems appropriate in the capital of the auto industry. From 1957-1961, the team plays at Olympia Stadium.

George Yardley leads the league in scoring with 27.8 points per game, a mark that would survive into the 1990s as the best in Pistons history. He also becomes the first player in league history to score 2,000 points in a season (2,001).

Olympia Stadium hosts the NBA All-Star Game on January 23 as the West defeats the East, 124-108.

doubleheaders, the league was a far cry from being an overnight success, primarily relying on two main attractions: George Mikan (of the Minneapolis Lakers) and the Harlem Globetrotters, who played the front end of doubleheaders in which an NBA game followed. The success of Zollner's business allowed him to provide

The Pistons would once again advance to the Finals the following season, but fell to the Philadelphia Warriors in five games.

In 1957-58, the franchise's first season in Detroit, Yardley, a sharp shooting forward, led the league in scoring with a 27.8 points per game average and became the first player in

---

"He was really disappointed. He said, 'I'm moving the team to Detroit.' And that's what he eventually did."

---

the league with much needed financial support, transportation assistance, as well as personnel to help keep it afloat during this tumultuous time.

Since the revenue streams for this new league weren't exactly flowing, the Pistons played the majority of their games at Fort Wayne's North High School. It wasn't until Zollner convinced the city to build an all-purpose arena that the Pistons would finally have a big-league home. The Pistons surged to the NBA Finals versus the Syracuse Nationals in 1955 and because no one in this northern Indiana city had expected them to reach the championship series, the arena was already booked, having previously scheduled a bowling tournament, forcing the Pistons to play Games 3, 4 and 5 in Indianapolis.

"He was really disappointed," said Nats' owner Danny Biasone of Zollner. "He said, 'I'm moving the team to Detroit.' And that's what he eventually did."

Featuring George Yardley, Max Zaslofsky and Mel Hutchins, the Pistons battled the Syracuse Nationals in a hard-fought seven-game series that featured plenty of great shots, great moves and plenty of fouls. It was also the first Finals that featured the shot clock, a league-saving innovation of which Zollner was a big proponent. Despite being up 17 points in Game 7 at Syracuse, Fort Wayne ended up losing in heartbreaking fashion as the Nationals' George King played a crucial role down the stretch, sinking one of two free throws and coming up with a clutch steal to seal the victory and championship.

NBA history to score 2,000 points in one season (2,001), breaking the 1,932-point record held by Mikan.

"He could get rid of the ball as quickly as anybody," Pistons coach Charlie Eckman said. "He wasn't big, but he could give that head fake. Bingo! The shot was up and gone."

As the Pistons moved into their new home, Cobo Arena, in 1961, they had reached the NBA playoffs 12 consecutive seasons. The streak reached 13, although Detroit eventually fell to Elgin Baylor, Jerry West and the Los Angeles Lakers in six games in the Western Division Finals. A local star at Austin Catholic High School and the University of Detroit, Dave DeBusschere was selected by the Pistons as a territorial pick in the 1962 NBA Draft. The 6-6 forward also excelled in baseball, having pitched for the Chicago White Sox in '62 and '63. At age 24, DeBusschere became the youngest coach in NBA history when he assumed the role of player-coach 11 games into the 1964-65 season.

The arrival of 6-3 guard Dave Bing in 1966 gave the Pistons another key component. Bing went on to win NBA Rookie of the Year honors and helped the Pistons average a franchise-best 118.6 points per game the following season while becoming the first guard since 1948 to lead the league in scoring. The Pistons ended up trading DeBusschere the following season to New York, where he would eventually help lead the Knicks to two titles in three seasons.

As the new decade approached, the franchise welcomed another great player to the Motor City. In 1970, Detroit

---

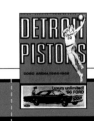

1961-66

In 1961-62 the Pistons begin playing their home games at Cobo Arena, where they would remain through the 1977-78 season. In 1962 the Pistons drafted hometown hero Dave DeBusschere. The 6-6, 235-pounder out of Austin Catholic Prep High School and the University of Detroit leads the Pistons in rebounding for three seasons, beginning in 1965-66. In 1964, DeBusschere serves as a player/coach at age 24, making him the youngest coach in league history.

1966-70

The Pistons select 6'3" guard Dave Bing with the No. 2 pick in the 1966 NBA Draft. Bing won NBA Rookie of the Year honors after averaging 20 points per game. The Washington, D.C. native leads the NBA in scoring in only his second season with a 27.1 mark. Bing would ultimately amass 18,327 points in 901 contests (20.3 ppg) in 12 NBA seasons, nine with Detroit.

Earl Lloyd becomes the league's first African-American assistant coach with the Pistons in 1968. Three seasons later, he would become the second African-American head coach in NBA history (12 games into Detroit's 1971-72 season).

1970-78

Detroit selects Bob Lanier, a 6'11" All-American from St. Bonaventure, with the top pick in the 1970 NBA Draft. He would play more than nine seasons in Detroit and remains the team's all-time leader in scoring average (22.7 ppg) and ranks second in rebounds (8,063) and third in points (15,488).

1974-76

William Davidson, a Detroit-area businessman, acquires the team from Fred Zollner. On January 15, 1974, Bob Lanier earns NBA All-Star Game MVP honors after scoring 24 points and grabbing 10 rebounds in leading the West to a 134-123 victory over the East.

1977-78

Dick Vitale was named the franchise's 18th head coach and guided the Pistons for the 1977-78 season and 12 games of the 79-80 season before being let go. He would later earn acclaim as one of college basketball's premiere basketball analysts for ESPN.

Bob Lanier is the fourth-ever recipient of the J.Walter Kennedy Citizenship Award.

selected Bob Lanier, a 6-11 big man who possessed an unstoppable sweeping left hook shot, a dominant inside game and a soft shooting touch from the perimeter. The St. Bonaventure star had injured his knee in an NCAA Regional Final against Villanova in his senior season, but despite the setback, the Pistons still selected the First-Team All-American with the first overall pick of the 1970 NBA Draft.

"Even though I was excited that somebody would take the chance on me, I was really concerned that I could live up to the expectations," said Lanier. "It took me a good two years to get my knee to full strength where I could regain my quickness and confidence. After that, I was rolling."

Lanier joined Bing in providing one of the NBA's most potent inside-outside combinations for five seasons before the six-time All-Star guard was traded to Washington following the 1974-75 season, the first under new owner

---

"It took me a good two years to get my knee to full strength where I could regain my quickness and confidence. After that, I was rolling."

BOB LANIER

Davidson, who purchased the team from Zollner. Lanier averaged better than 20 points and 10 rebounds from 1974 to 1978, leading the Pistons to the postseason in three of those seasons. Early playoff exits and revolving coaches, however, became the norm during his tenure. During his 10 seasons in Detroit, the perennial All-Star played under eight different coaches, including Earl Lloyd, who became only the second African-American in NBA history to call the shots from an NBA bench. Before moving on to Milwaukee, Lanier accumulated a multitude of franchise records, including the highest scoring average (22.7 ppg), second-highest rebound total (8,063) and third-highest point total (15,488).

As the 1980s approached, the Pistons hit rock-bottom with a franchise-worst 16-66 record in the 1978-79 season, their first in the Pontiac Silverdome. Fortunately, hope and optimism and a new era of winning were right around

the corner with the arrival of 6-1 point guard, Isiah Thomas. The No. 2 overall pick of the 1982 NBA Draft, Thomas was fresh from leading Indiana University to the NCAA title as a sophomore and it didn't take he and fellow rookie Kelly Tripucka long to point the Pistons in the right direction. Soon, other key individuals arrived, gradually laying the championship foundation. The following season, the team acquired center Bill Laimbeer via a trade with the Cleveland Cavaliers and in 1983 Chuck Daly came on board as coach. Two years later, the team drafted a little-known 6-3 guard out of McNeese State named Joe Dumars with the 18th overall pick.

The Pistons began climbing the NBA ladder, ranking among the Central Division elite as Thomas and Dumars formed one of the best backcourt duos in the NBA while the team featured instant offense off the bench from Vinnie "The Microwave" Johnson, who always seemed to be heating up. Adrian Dantley, who was acquired in a trade from Utah, gave the team another highly effective scoring option. The Pistons advanced to the 1987 Eastern Conference Finals (the first time in 25 years they had done so) and lost a crucial Game 5 at Boston Garden when Larry Bird stole an inbounds pass from Thomas and spotted teammate Dennis Johnson for the game-winning layup. It was a heartbreaking loss and, even though the Pistons would win Game 6, they lost Game 7 in Boston.

Detroit bounced back the following season, winning the Central Division for the first time in franchise history as the Pistons cemented their reputation as one of the NBA's premier rebounding and defensive teams. The "Bad Boys," led by Laimbeer, Rick Mahorn and Dennis Rodman, formed an imposing frontline as the team advanced to the NBA Finals versus the Los Angeles Lakers. Although the Pistons lost in seven games, the 1988 series featured one of the greatest individual performances of all time when Thomas set a Finals scoring record for most points in a quarter with 25 despite being hobbled with a sprained right ankle.

The 1988-89 season welcomed the opening of a new state-of-the-art arena that served as the standard for all future NBA venues. The Palace of Auburn Hills featured the latest amenities and a capacity of more than 22,000 as the Pistons christened their palatial building in style. Built around solid frontcourt players and sharp-shooting

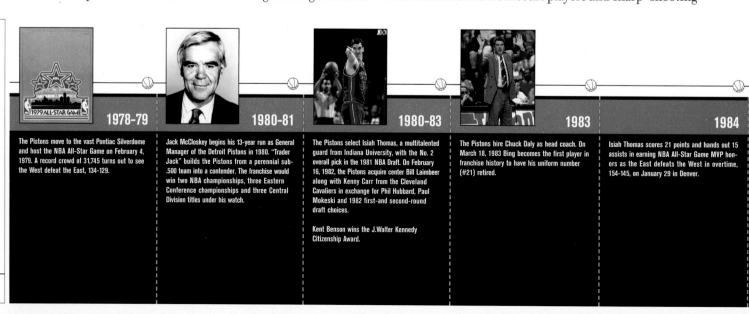

1978-79

The Pistons move to the vast Pontiac Silverdome and host the NBA All-Star Game on February 4, 1979. A record crowd of 31,745 turns out to see the West defeat the East, 134-129.

1980-81

Jack McCloskey begins his 13-year run as General Manager of the Detroit Pistons in 1980. "Trader Jack" builds the Pistons from a perennial sub-.500 team into a contender. The franchise would win two NBA championships, three Eastern Conference championships and three Central Division titles under his watch.

1980-83

The Pistons select Isiah Thomas, a multitalented guard from Indiana University, with the No. 2 overall pick in the 1981 NBA Draft. On February 16, 1982, the Pistons acquire center Bill Laimbeer along with Kenny Carr from the Cleveland Cavaliers in exchange for Phil Hubbard, Paul Mokeski and 1982 first-and second-round draft choices.

Kent Benson wins the J.Walter Kennedy Citizenship Award.

1983

The Pistons hire Chuck Daly as head coach. On March 18, 1983 Bing becomes the first player in franchise history to have his uniform number (#21) retired.

1984

Isiah Thomas scores 21 points and hands out 15 assists in earning NBA All-Star Game MVP honors as the East defeats the West in overtime, 154-145, on January 29 in Denver.

1985

The Pistons select 6'3" guard Joe Dumars out of McNeese State in 1985 NBA Draft, securing the third member of a triumvirate (with Laimbeer and Thomas) that will anchor their championship teams of the future. Thomas becomes the fourth player in NBA history to amass more than 9,000 assists, averaging 13.9 assists per game that season.

1986

Isiah Thomas earns his second NBA All-Star Game MVP Award in three years as he scores 30 points along with 10 assists to lead the East to a 139-132 victory over the West on February 9 in Dallas.

1986-87

Isiah Thomas wins the J.Walter Kennedy Citizenship Award.

1987-88

The Pistons advance to the NBA Finals for the first time in more than 30 years, losing to the Los Angeles Lakers in seven games. Detroit, which sets a franchise record with 54 regular-season wins, also establishes an attendance mark when 61,983 fans turn out at the Pontiac Silverdome to see the rival Boston Celtics visit on January 29, 1988. An NBA Finals record 41,732 fans watched as the Pistons defeat the Lakers in Game 5 of the Finals, 104-94.

1988-89

The Pistons moves to the 21,454-seat Palace of Auburn Hills and soon reaches the top of the basketball world, with a four game sweep of the Los Angeles Lakers in the NBA Finals. The Pistons also set a franchise-best 63-regular season wins on the way to the Central Division title. Joe Dumars wins NBA Finals MVP honors.

MIKE ABDENOUR

HERB BROWN

guards, the Pistons were on a mission that season, holding opponents to 100.8 points per game. Reluctant to embrace Daly's uptempo offensive game, Dantley was traded for Mark Aguirre, a former No. 1 overall pick, who averaged 15.5 points for the remainder of the season as Detroit returned to the Finals.

"We have an unusually large number of mentally strong players on this team," said Laimbeer. "Make no mistake — we did learn from Boston the past few years about how far mental toughness can carry you. They were the champions of that every year."

In a rematch of the '88 Finals, the Pistons weren't going to be denied, sweeping the Lakers, who lost Byron Scott and Magic Johnson to hamstring injuries, as Dumars went on to earn MVP honors.

"It means so much, so much," said Thomas following the Pistons' Game 4 triumph. "Winning four [in the Finals] is much sweeter after you lost four. Believe me."

The Pistons posted the NBA's second-best record the following season and defeated the upstart Chicago Bulls in a seven-game series in the Eastern Conference Finals to return to their third consecutive Finals appearance.

Despite winning the title in 1988, many of the Pistons felt they hadn't received their proper due because of the injuries suffered by the two key Lakers in the Finals. Out

to prove their critics wrong, the Pistons faced the Portland Trail Blazers and their superstar guard Clyde Drexler in the 1990 Finals. After splitting the first two games, Detroit went on to win the next three and were led by Thomas' 27.6 points series average, which earned him the Finals MVP award. After the league had gone 19 years without repeat champions, the Pistons won back-to-back titles following the Lakers' accomplishment.

"You rank this one as more of a satisfaction for a job well done," said Laimbeer. "We wanted to repeat as champions, but not so much to prove it to anybody else. We wanted to do it for ourselves."

As the 1990s unfolded, the Pistons underwent a period of transition, which saw Daly, who had amassed 538 victories, depart to coach the New Jersey Nets while Thomas and Laimbeer soon retired and Rodman eventually was traded to the San Antonio Spurs. Dumars remained the link to the team's glorious past as Detroit welcomed a cornerstone in Duke All-American forward Grant Hill in 1994, as the team aimed to return to the playoffs after a three-year drought. As first-round exits became the norm, Dumars retired and assumed control of the team's basketball operations in 2000 and through a series of player personnel and coaching moves masterfully rebuilt the Pistons back to championship level. ◯

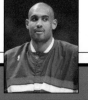

1989-1990

Detroit repeats as NBA champions, defeating the Portland Trail Blazers in five games as Isiah Thomas wins NBA Finals MVP honors.

1991-92

Dennis Rodman leads the NBA in rebounding with 18.7 boards per game, while setting new team standards for most rebounds (1,530), most offensive rebounds (523), and most defensive rebounds (1,007) in a season.

1992-1993

On January 9, Hall of Famer Bob Lanier becomes the second player in franchise history to have his uniform number (#16) retired.

Bill Laimbeer pulled down his 10,000th career rebound against the Philadelphia 76ers on December 5, becoming the 19th player in NBA history to record 10,000 points and 10,000 rebounds. By the end of the 1992-93 season, Laimbeer had become the team's all-time leading rebounder.

1994

Isiah Thomas retires at age 33, ending his playing career with 9,061 assists in 979 games (9.3 apg). Joe Dumars wins the J. Walter Kennedy Citizenship Award while Vinnie Johnson becomes the third player in franchise history to have his uniform number (#15) retired on February 5. The Pistons select Duke University forward Grant Hill with the third overall selection of the 1994 NBA Draft. Hill goes on to share NBA Rookie of the Year honors with Dallas' Jason Kidd.

1995

Grant Hill emerges as the team's top scorer at 19.9 points per game, becoming the first rookie ever to lead all players in fan voting for the NBA All-Star Game. On February 4, Bill Laimbeer becomes the fourth player in franchise history to have his uniform number (#40) retired.

On February 17, Isiah Thomas becomes the fifth player in franchise history to have his uniform number (#11) retired.

In celebration of its 50th anniversary, the NBA announces the 50 Greatest Players in NBA History, which was voted by an expert panel. Dave DeBusschere, Dave Bing and Thomas were selected while Chuck Daly was named one of the Top 10 Coaches in NBA History. The 1988-89 Pistons ranked among the top 10 teams in NBA History. On January 25, the team retires No. 2 in honor of Chuck Daly coaching the Pistons to two championships.

1996-97

On May 16, Joe Dumars announces his retirement from a 14-year playing career spent entirely with the Pistons after a first round playoff exit to the Atlanta Hawks.

1999

On March 10, Joe Dumars becomes the sixth player in franchise history to have his uniform number (#4) retired. During the ceremony, the NBA announces that the Sportsmanship Award has been renamed to the Joe Dumars Trophy. On June 6, he is named the team's President of Basketball Operations.

Ben Wallace becomes the first Piston to win the NBA's Defensive of the Player of the Year Honors. Coach Rick Carlisle helps the team to a 50-32 record and the Central Division title.

George Blaha marks his 25th consecutive season as the television and radio play-by-play voice of the Pistons.

2000-01

Joe Dumars wins NBA Executive of the Year honors while Ben Wallace wins his second consecutive NBA Defensive Player of the Year honor and Corliss Williamson receives the NBA's Sixth Man of the Year Award. The team claims a second consecutive Central Division title at 50-32.

2002-03

Head coach Larry Brown, a Hall-of-Fame inductee in his first year with the franchise, directs the Pistons to their third NBA championship, shocking the Los Angeles Lakers in five games. Detroit's record-setting defense is highlighted by 11 games in which the Pistons hold opponents under 70 points, including a five-game stretch in early March that establishes an NBA mark, since the inception of the 24-second shot clock in 1954-55.

On February 27, 2004, the Pistons honor Will Robinson, a Detroit coaching legend, for his 28 years of service as a team scout. It was Robinson who first urged the team to draft Joe Dumars out of McNeese State.

2003-04

CHAMPIONS

In a culture that celebrates individual virtuosity, the Detroit Pistons are the new universal barometer for team work. They're the symbol of hard work, selflessness and excellence. The impact of Detroit's championship and the way the Pistons accomplished their mission has far-reaching implications beyond the sports world. The premise of togetherness with everyone working toward

The Pistons are already the best as thousands of fans gathered along the 1.3 mile parade route along Jefferson Avenue celebrating their newly minted status as NBA champions. From Chene Park all the way to Hart Plaza, fans flocked – a dozen deep in many sections — overflowing the curbs as they cheered their heroes as each one slowly drifted by, perched atop of the back seat of a

"Yes sir! Yes sir! Yes sir! We got a great group of guys and the thing about us is we're young, we're hungry. This ain't going to be the last one. There's still food for us to eat and we're gonna keep bringing them back to the D. Yes sir!"

RICHARD HAMILTON

the same goal is a model for any group or organization aspiring to achieve the ultimate success.

One such example was chronicled in a recent *New York Times* article in which the chief executive of J.P. Morgan Chase, William B. Harrison Jr., spoke to a roomful of executives about an impending merger with Bank One and the keys to a successful partnership. Looking for inspiration, Harrison cited the Pistons as the standard-bearer for team work.

"The Pistons didn't have anyone," said Harrison. "A team beats superstars every time — that's execution. The difference between good and great is going to be execution. Let's be the best."

Corvette convertible waving to their admirers. Fans of all ages were decked out in their favorite Pistons attire. A sea of No. 3 jerseys and fake fros all waved in unison as Ben Wallace, accompanied by his family, made his way through, proudly clutching the Larry O'Brien Trophy for all to see.

When he wasn't waving to the fans, Richard Hamilton, wearing a No. 32 Rip City jersey, was feverishly signing t-shirts before tossing them into the crowd as the masses instantly swallowed them up. Several cars ahead, Rasheed Wallace, looking relaxed in his No. 9 Gordie Howe Red Wings jersey, flashed the peace sign when he wasn't throwing souvenirs to the fans who embraced him ever since his arrival on February 19. Overwhelmed with the

affection he and his teammates were receiving, Wallace was quite content.

"I don't have words for it," said Wallace. "I'm just feeling all good inside."

As the parade of cars pulled in to Hart Plaza, an estimate one million fans were waiting for their heroes. Shouts of "De-troit basket-ballll" were prevalent as signs dotted the scene:

Don't Flee the D Sheed … Kobe Got Rip'd ….. We earned our respect … Most Valuable Player --- Mr. Big Shot – Chauncey Billups

George Blaha, the legendary voice of Pistons basketball for the past 28 years, served as Master of Ceremonies, introducing everyone from the Governor of Michigan Jennifer Granholm, the Mayor of Detroit, Kwame Kilpatrick to members of the coaching staff, players and William Davidson, the soft-spoken owner who cleared a few things off his chest:

"Over the past couple of weeks, there's been a lot of bull---- going on in this country. Let me be a little more refined and say misconception. Let's start with the 8-1 odds on the Lakers to beat the Pistons. Bull----. Actually, they were lucky to win one game."

The crowd roared in delight.

Later that afternoon, the party shifted over to The Palace of Auburn Hills as 25,000 anxious fans welcomed each team member and coach to center court where Blaha once again led the proceedings. Larry Brown, the well-traveled

"They were lucky to win one game."

WILLIAM DAVIDSON
Owner, Detroit Pistons

coach and the only man to have won an NCAA and NBA championship, addressed the jubilant crowd.

"Everybody knows that I've been to a lot of places, and I've enjoyed coaching in a lot of different cities," said Brown. "But never have I been in a place that the fans are more loyal and more supportive and care more about the team than right here in Detroit."

It was official. Hockeytown had been converted to Hoopstown on this overcast, humid day as Hamilton stoked the crowd, entertaining thoughts of future celebrations for a Pistons team that should contend for years to come.

"Yes sir! Yes sir! Yes sir!" exclaimed Hamilton. "I just want to end on this, man. We got a great group of guys and the thing about us is we're young and we're hungry. This ain't going to be the last one. There's still food for us to eat and we're gonna keep bringing them back to the D.

Yes sir!"

LARRY BROWN

The roots of coaching greatness first took hold during the summer of 1962. Twenty-one-year-old Larry Brown had just completed his junior season at the University of North Carolina and spent his summer volunteering at a camp in Pennsylvania. Upon completion of his first official foray into coaching, the point guard couldn't wait to share the news with his coach about his future career path.

"He called me to say his team won the championship and he wanted to coach," said Dean Smith, who gave Brown his

"The people that I learned from made me aware on a daily basis that we had to play the right way," said Brown on where he inherited his philosophy. "Basically, play unselfishly, play hard and try to make your teammates better. I think that's one thing since I've been coaching we've always tried to do."

The team-first philosophy ingrained from his days in Chapel Hill served Brown and his teams well as he has compiled one of the most impressive basketball coaching

"He's pretty demanding. He cares about winning and he truly cares about the guys."

CHAUNCEY BILLUPS

first coaching job as an assistant with the Tar Heels in 1965. "He had them running the shuffle offense, which is really complicated. They were undefeated in camp play and he was smitten at that point with the idea of being a coach."

Although Brown's goal of playing professionally was ultimately derailed, which he did for five seasons as an All-Star point guard in the American Basketball Association, that experience served as a springboard to a lifelong journey of coaching excellence that eventually took him to the collegiate, professional and international levels and all over the world to camps and clinics, teaching the fundamentals of playing the right way.

résumés in the history of the game. Over the course of 32 years, Brown has collected more than 1,300 wins, an NCAA Championship, four Coach of the Year Awards (three in the ABA, one in the NBA), led a record seven different NBA teams to the playoffs and gained membership into basketball's most exclusive fraternity, the Naismith Memorial Basketball Hall of Fame, in 2002. He is also the only person to win an Olympic gold medal as a player and as an assistant coach. His latest accomplishment, leading the Detroit Pistons to the NBA championship allows him to lay claim to being the only head coach ever to win both an NCAA and an NBA title. Brown will go for the unprece-

dented trifecta this summer as coach of the U.S. Men's Senior National Team in Athens.

The lineage of basketball people who influenced Brown began at a young age while growing up in Long Beach, N.Y. Living on top of his grandfather's bakery, Brown met Red Holzman and other members of the New York Knicks, who practiced at a playground across the street near the boardwalk. It was there where he began learning about the importance of finding the open man, moving without the ball and playing team defense, all necessary elements of playing the game the right way. There was Frank McGuire and Smith at North Carolina, Henry Iba and John McClendon with the 1964 U.S. gold-medal winning Olympic team, Alex Hannum with the Denver Rockets and along the way, other great basketball minds such as Pete Newell, all of whom left an indelible impression on the 5-9 guard. Their influence in how Brown approaches and teaches the game, how his

> ## "If Larry never played a game, he would be happy if he could just practice everyday and teach the game."
>
> GREGG POPOVICH

teams prepare and why he is ultimately known as a perfectionist, is undeniable.

"He's pretty demanding," said Pistons point guard Chauncey Billups. "He gets a little crazy sometimes, but we always know that it's all about the game. He only wants to win and that's the bottom line, and he wants to make you a better player. No agendas, nothing like that. He cares about winning and he truly cares about the guys. When he's going crazy and things like that, you can respect it more than anything because you know that he cares."

The compassion Brown exhibits is not solely limited to his players, but extends to the basketball community as well. The list of individuals who Brown has mentored over the years is a who's who of movers and shakers in today's NBA: Gregg Popovich (head coach, San Antonio Spurs), Byron Scott (head coach, New Orleans Hornets), Alvin Gentry (assistant coach, Phoenix Suns), R.C. Buford (General Manager, Spurs), Billy King (President and GM of the Philadelphia 76ers) and Kevin O'Connor (Senior Vice President of Basketball Operations, Utah Jazz).

The practice of coaches turning out coaches, positively influencing the careers of men who chose to devote their life to the game of basketball; It's something Smith, Iba and McClendon all did and it's something Brown continues to do.

2004 NBA CHAMPIONS DETROIT PISTONS

28

			NBA	NBA
ENSHRINED IN NAISMITH MEMORIAL BASKETBALL HALL OF FAME (2002)	**10** HEAD-COACHING JOBS	**28** WINNING RECORDS IN 32 SEASONS	**7** RECORD NUMBER OF NBA FRANCHISES LED TO PLAYOFFS	**933** REGULAR-SEASON VICTORIES
NBA	**NBA**	**NBA**	**NBA**	**ABA**
1 NBA CHAMPIONSHIP (DETROIT PISTONS, 2004)	**.556** REGULAR-SEASON WINNING PERCENTAGE	**1** COACH OF THE YEAR (2001)	**2** CONFERENCE CHAMPIONSHIPS (2001, 2004)	**229** REGULAR-SEASON VICTORIES
ABA	**ABA**	**ABA**	**COLLEGE**	**COLLEGE**
.682 REGULAR-SEASON WINNING PERCENTAGE	**3** COACH OF THE YEAR (1973, 1975, 1976)	**5** ALL-STAR GAMES AS A PLAYER, (ALL-STAR GAME MVP IN 1968)	**1** NCAA MEN'S CHAMPIONSHIP (UNIVERSITY OF KANSAS, 1988)	**177** NCAA REGULAR-SEASON VICTORIES
COLLEGE	**OLYMPICS**	**OLYMPICS**	**OLYMPICS**	**OLYMPICS**
.744 NCAA REGULAR-SEASON WINNING PERCENTAGE	**1964** GOLD MEDAL (PLAYER) U.S. MEN'S SENIOR NATIONAL TEAM	**1980** (ASSISTANT COACH) U.S. MEN'S SENIOR NATIONAL TEAM	**2000** GOLD MEDAL (ASST. COACH) U.S. MEN'S SENIOR NATIONAL TEAM	**2004** HEAD COACH U.S. MEN'S SENIOR NATIONAL TEAM

"I owe my basketball career to Larry Brown."

ALVIN GENTRY

"I owe my basketball career to Larry Brown," said Gentry who served as an assistant coach on Brown's staff at the University of Kansas the year they won the NCAA title. "The reason that I am where I am right now is because of Larry."

The first order of business Popovich had on opening night of the 1999-00 season, when he received his NBA championship ring, was walk over to the opposing team's sideline and hand the piece of jewelry over to the man who gave him an opportunity as a volunteer assistant coach at Kansas before eventually hiring him with the Spurs.

"I wouldn't be here without him," said Popovich, one of only 12 men in NBA history with two or more rings. "He's had a huge impact on what I believe about the game, what wins and what loses, how to play the game."

Brown earned his reputation as one of the game's premier teachers with his ability to transform losing teams into contenders virtually overnight. With the Pistons, he took a contender and elevated them to the top of the NBA. So, while winning an NBA title completes a brilliant career, the legacy of this basketball purist transcends any statistic or championship. It boils down to the same passion that fueled an aspiring 21-year-old at a basketball summer camp in Pennyslvania 42 years ago.

"I think he'll be remembered as someone who really loved the game because of what it stood for and how beautiful it can be when played correctly," said Popovich. "He cares about that. If Larry never played a game, he would be happy if he could just practice every day and teach the game. I think that's what people are going to think of when they think of Larry Brown."

2004 NBA CHAMPIONS DETROIT PISTONS

CHAUNCEY BILLUPS

Boston. Toronto. Denver. Orlando. Minnesota. Detroit. Six teams in seven years. Not exactly the stable career path envisioned by a No. 3 overall pick in the 1997 NBA Draft, but that was the course taken by Chauncey Billups, the former University of Colorado star.

"The way my career had gone, it seemed like my chance was kind of drifting away," said Billups.

averaging a career best 16.2 points per game. When Larry Brown arrived prior to the 2003-04 season, Billups learned to adjust his game for a coach who is known to expect a lot from his point guards.

"One thing I've learned from Coach Brown is knowing that I don't have to take a lot of shots in some games to be as effective, and that's one of the beautiful things that

> ## "I never gave up on what I felt I could do. And what I felt I could do is win the Championship and have a chance to win this trophy right here. I never stopped dreaming."
>
> CHAUNCEY BILLUPS

The opportunity to prove himself presented itself in his fourth season when he averaged 15.1 points, 6.6 assists and 3.4 rebounds in 54 games as a starter for the Minnesota Timberwolves, filling in for the injured Terrell Brandon. It was then when Joe Dumars, the Pistons' President of Basketball Operations, felt Billups could find a home running Detroit's offense.

"Once he became a free agent, I made an all-out pitch to get this guy," said Dumars. "I just felt that if he's in the right situation — put the ball in his hands, don't have him looking over his shoulder — that he's going to be a good player. And he proved it."

Dumars did get his man after Billups' second season in Minnesota, signing the 6-3 point guard to a six-year contract. Billups excelled in his first season in Motown,

Coach has taught me, and I've bought into that and I really believe it now," he said.

Billups heeded Brown's advice by shooting less and distributing more, especially in the second half of the season as Detroit emerged as a championship contender. Yet Billups didn't hesitate to go to his strength in the Finals when Los Angeles allowed him to score at will, feasting on pick-and-roll situations, as he sliced the Lakers defense to the tune of 21 points on 51 percent shooting, netting him MVP honors.

"I never gave up," said Billups after Game 5 of the Finals. "I never gave up on what I felt I could do. And what I felt I could do is win the Championship and have a chance to win this trophy right here. I never stopped dreaming."

RICHARD HAMILTON

He is one of the NBA's fastest rising young stars. A special player who elevates his game during the bright lights and global stage of the NBA Playoffs. Few players can handle the pressure, demand the ball and hit clutch jumpers with such frequency as this 6-6 shooting guard. Few players relish the big moment like Richard Hamilton.

"I love the postseason," said Hamilton. "I've loved it since college. And I never got a chance to play in it again until Detroit."

from good to great and that helped me a lot," said the man nicknamed "Rip."

Hamilton's development didn't go unnoticed by Joe Dumars, Detroit's President of Basketball Operations, who saw a lot of potential in the third-year player.

"I had looked at him before that season in Washington and remembered saying, 'Man, if I could only get that kid right there,'" said Dumars, who traded Jerry Stackhouse, the league's leading scorer, to acquire Hamilton. "I knew

> ## "Hamilton is a tireless worker and capable of being a one-man wrecking crew out there."
>
> PHIL JACKSON

It was an excruciating four-year wait for the Coatesville, Pa., native. After leading the University of Connecticut to the 1999 NCAA Championship, Hamilton was selected with the seventh overall pick of the NBA Draft three months later by the Washington Wizards. Three consecutive lottery-bound seasons didn't get Hamilton any closer to his favorite destination. Yet, despite the losing, Hamilton's development from mid-range specialist to all-around player began to take root in his third season, playing alongside the legendary Michael Jordan. Suddenly, Hamilton was moving without the ball with greater fervor, creating opportunities for himself while observing Jordan's mental and defensive approach to the game.

"Playing with MJ taught me a lot of things about going

he was going to be good. He's only going to improve."

Hamilton blossomed in his first NBA postseason, averaging 22.5 points per game, three above his regular-season mark. The evolution continued in this season's playoffs as Rip once again led the team in scoring, accounting for 26 percent of the total offense while signs of a well-rounded game were evident in his assist and steal totals, ranking second in both.

"He's always been a scorer," said Pistons coach Larry Brown. "But he's become more of a complete player. He's gotten better defensively. He's become a much better passer."

The transition from one-dimensional player to emerging superstar is now officially complete for this prime-time postseason performer. ♫

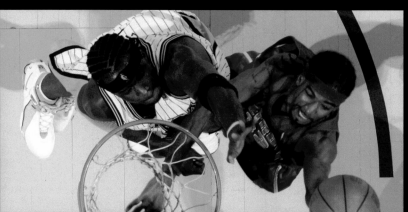

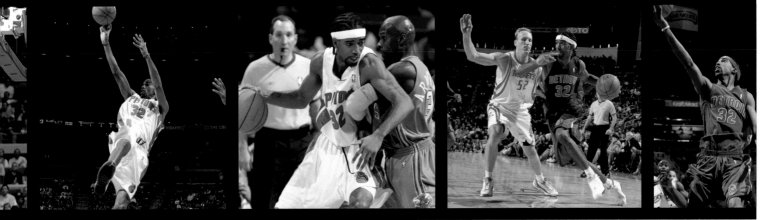

2004 NBA CHAMPIONS DETROIT PISTONS

BEN WALLACE

He went from undrafted rookie to sports icon but Ben Wallace is hardly considered an overnight sensation. The pride of White Hall, Ala., took the long road to NBA superstardom via Cuyahoga Community College (Ohio), Virginia Union and the Italian Basketball League before receiving a call from Washington Bullets' General Manager Wes Unseld. Since then, Wallace's career has been on a steady upward climb, thanks to a relentless work ethic and a tenacity to

things come to those who wait, keep working hard and hope good things happen and *it's easier to appreciate things you earn than things you are given.*

It is an approach that has garnered Wallace his share of admirers, including his current coach, Larry Brown.

"When I was an outsider, I just marveled at how well he played," said Brown. "Now, being around him, you know, he does things that just blow you away. He's got good feet,

---

> ## "He's the foundation. This team has been built in the image of Ben. We're hard working and we don't complain. Everything we do starts with him."
>
> JOE DUMARS

---

grab every rebound and block every shot within his bulging biceps' radius. After a breakthrough season with the Orlando Magic in 1999-2000, newly-minted President of Basketball Operations, Joe Dumars, acquired the 6-9 center in exchange for Grant Hill in a deal that ultimately set the Pistons on a championship course.

"He's the foundation," said Dumars. "This team has been built in the image of Ben. We're hard working and we don't complain. Everything we do starts with him. Having Ben is a great luxury and we flat-out love him here in Detroit."

The two-time NBA Defensive Player of the Year credits his late mother, Sadie, for inspiring him to greatness with a hard work, no-nonsense approach by instilling values that he lives by to this day. Maxims such as *good*

he's got great hands defensively, and he's relentless."

Thanks to Brown, Wallace expanded his game, displaying considerable offensive muscle. Big Ben averaged a career high in points (9.5) and saved his finest offensive outing for the Game 5 Finals clincher against the Los Angeles Lakers, scoring 18 points along with his 22 rebounds. Not bad for a player who scored 20 points only once in his NBA career — five years ago.

Despite the expanded offensive game, Wallace's bread and butter begins and ends with his stifling defense.

"I'm just proud to be able to go out there and protect our basket. Whichever one it takes, blocks, steals, rebounding or whatever, I'm just glad to be out there being able to protect the basket and being able to give the team the opportunity to win."

TAYSHAUN PRINCE

The question wouldn't go away. It persisted and lingered throughout the 82-game season: Why didn't the Pistons select Carmelo Anthony, the impact player out of Syracuse with the No. 2 overall pick in the 2003 NBA Draft? It was a topic that picked up steam as Anthony was injecting new life into a perennial lottery-bound franchise, the Denver Nuggets, leading them to the NBA Playoffs while stockpiling NBA Rookie of the Month honors along the way. It appeared to be a clear-cut choice to everyone but Joe Dumars, the chief decision maker and

coming-out party in the first-round series against the Orlando Magic in the 2003 playoffs when he shut down the NBA's leading scorer, Tracy McGrady, in Game 5, Prince once again elevated his game with sterling defensive performances throughout Detroit's march to the championship through Milwaukee, New Jersey and Indiana. How suffocating was Prince's defense? His opponents' shooting percentages tell the story: Desmond Mason – 33 percent; Richard Jefferson – 42 percent and Ron Artest – 30 percent.

> ## "We never thought Tayshaun Prince was notably a defensive stopper, but all of a sudden he is. He's on top of Kobe, playing him very, very well."
>
> PHIL JACKSON

architect of the Pistons, who instead opted for 7-1 forward-center Darko Milicic out of Serbia. After all, why select a small forward when one resides on your roster by the name of Tayshaun Prince, a player with a huge upside?

"It was a confidence booster knowing that the GM has a lot of faith in me to go out there and play the way I've been playing and what I'm accustomed to doing," said Prince. "The coaching staff showed the same type of confidence and it paid off."

It sure did. Prince made the transition from bench player in his rookie season to starter in his second and it reflected in his numbers, which received a spike across the board. But the real breakthrough for the University of Kentucky graduate was the postseason. Similar to his

The soft-spoken Compton, Calif., native saved his most impressive defensive effort for the biggest stage of them all, the NBA Finals, when he hounded and frustrated one of the NBA's premier players, Kobe Bryant, into his worst Finals shooting performance ever. Bryant struggled from the field, shooting 38 percent, including a shocking 17 percent from the three-point line.

"We never thought Tayshaun Prince was notably a defensive stopper, but all of a sudden he is," said Lakers coach Phil Jackson. "He's on top of Kobe, playing him very, very well. That's how [players] generate to become superstars."

Tayshaun is on his way, in a quiet, non-boastful manner. Now, what was that question regarding who the Pistons should have drafted?

RASHEED WALLACE

He was the championship difference. A player with an edge and a stellar all-around game who arrived in Detroit and transformed a good team into a great one. How valuable was Rasheed Wallace to the Pistons? When Detroit acquired him in a trade on February 19, the Pistons were 34-22. Two months later, Detroit rolled to a 20-6 finish and compiled a 16-7 record in the postseason en route to the franchise's first title in 14 years.

further, holding opponents to 73.4 points while enjoying a whopping 15.6 point differential. Detroit turned in other defensive gems such as setting an NBA record of holding 11 teams under 70 points, eight of which were set after Wallace hit town, including a record-setting five in a row. The Pistons also set a franchise mark of holding opponents to 84.3 points per game, which also ranks as a league mark since the shot clock was invented 49 years ago.

> ## "He made our whole team better in every way. There's no way I would be standing up here, or any of us would have been in this kind of situation without him."
>
> LARRY BROWN after the Game 5 Finals clincher

"He made our whole team better in every way," said Pistons coach Larry Brown after the Game 5 Finals clincher. "I think most people felt when he came here that he was going to be an offensive force, and he was in a lot of ways. But his presence defensively with Ben [Wallace] and Tayshaun [Prince] gave us unbelievable shot-blocking, quickness, unselfish play. There's no way I would be standing up here, or any of us would have been in this kind of situation without him."

Thanks to Wallace, Detroit's stingy defense soon became legendary. Prior to the 6-11 power forward's arrival, the Pistons' D held opponents to 85.5 points in victories with a point differential of 8.5. Since 'Sheed donned the red, white and blue uniform, the Pistons clamped down even

"That's why I went and got him," said Joe Dumars, Detroit's President of Basketball Operations. "I thought we were a contender to go deep in the playoffs without him. But once we got him, I thought he could be the piece that gets us over the hump to win this thing."

Ask Wallace about his enormous impact and he shrugs it off, downplaying his role as the missing championship piece.

"Before I got here this was already a good ballclub," said Wallace. "They already won 50-something games the last three years. So, it's not me. I bring a couple of points in as far as defense and offense. Just a couple percentage points higher. But it's the same core guys."

Plus one championship difference-maker.

TEAM

They are the ultimate blue-collar performers. Role players whose contributions are an invaluable and integral component to the Detroit Pistons' championship success. While other players garner the headlines, these minute-to-minute specialists routinely rise to the occasion. Want proof? Look no further than basketball's biggest stage – the NBA Finals – when they stepped up as they had done all season long. Whether it was Lindsey Hunter or Jon Barry, Michael Curry and Chucky Atkins and Bob Sura during the midseason while another — Tayshaun Prince — was elevated to the starting lineup. The new acquisitions consisted of tested veterans Hunter, Campbell and James as well as rookie Darko Milicic.

For Campbell, who was a starter for most of his career, accepting a limited role to be a part of something special was worth the sacrifice.

> "There's no shame in taking pride in being a supporting cast member. We have to have our superstars, our stars, and we count on them and we rely on them, so whenever we can help them out. That's when we're doing our job."
>
> ELDEN CAMPBELL

Mike James — the "pit bulls"— pressuring the ball and frustrating the Lakers' guards, Elden Campbell putting a body on Shaquille O'Neal or Mehmet Okur and Corliss Williamson providing instant offense, these men are the embodiment of the team slogan, "Hard Work Pays Off."

"It definitely lifts the confidence of everybody on the team," said Rasheed Wallace. "When the first five is out there, we have the bench supporting us, they are cheering and everything. And then when a couple of guys from the bench go in there, it's vice versa. They're ready. They are just as hyped as we are when we go into the game, so the bench definitely plays a big part of the series."

The supporting cast underwent somewhat of a transformation this past season, losing four valuable members in

"I wasn't playing as much as I would have liked to be playing, but it was enough that I'm a part of this team," said Campbell, who averaged 13.7 minutes during the season and 13.6 during the Finals. "There's no shame in taking pride in being a supporting cast member. We have to have our superstars, our stars, and we count on them and we rely on them, so whenever we can help them out. That's when we're doing our job."

Hunter, the 6-2 point guard, rejoined the team that had drafted him in 1993 and where he spent the first seven seasons of his career. Acquired prior to training camp, Hunter was part of the three-team midseason trade that landed Rasheed Wallace in Detroit and sent the Utica, Miss., native to the Boston Celtics. Recognizing the leadership, defensive

> "Elden Campbell, Corliss, Lindsey, people like that, give you a chance to be successful, whether they play 10 minutes or not."
>
> LARRY BROWN

abilities and intangibles he brings, the Pistons wasted no time in re-acquiring the veteran guard once he was released a week after the trade.

"He's a great on-ball defender," said Pistons coach Larry Brown. "He's got unbelievable toughness."

Hunter's backcourt partner and other half of the "pit bulls" tandem, James, was also part of the same deal, arriving from Boston. The 6-2 guard out of Duquesne started 55 games for the Celtics this season and had to make the adjustment of coming off the bench as he watched his minutes dip by 11 per game.

"I haven't handled Mike James the right way," said Brown during the Finals. "He has not had the opportunity to play a lot, but he is a big part of this team. He went from being a starter, playing major minutes, to sacrificing a lot of that with us. When you put him in the game, he gives you everything he's got. His defensive effort is phenomenal. And he's a great teammate."

While Milicic averaged only 4.7 minutes per game, the Pistons are high on his potential and were able to take their time in developing the Serbian native. Another international player, Okur, a native of Turkey, made the most of his second season, starting 33 games and averaging 9.6 points and 6 rebounds per game in 22 minutes of action. Darvin Ham, in his first season in Motown, averaged nine minutes per game.

Williamson, the "Big Nasty," once again provided consistency off the bench, averaging 9.5 points in 20 minutes of action and typified the mindset and approach taken by the veterans who more than fulfilled their roles this season.

"I think when you look around our league, there's a lot of older guys that are really professional guys that respect the game, respect their teammates and will do anything they can to make a contribution," said Brown. "A lot of times they understand it themselves and a lot of times as a staff, you ask them to do it and they make sacrifices.

"Elden Campbell, Corliss, Lindsey, people like that, give you a chance to be successful, whether they play 10 minutes or not."

SEASON

The quest for the Larry O'Brien Trophy began on October 29, 2003 as old and new faces converged on opening night at The Palace of Auburn Hills. It was an evening filled with celebration, anticipation and a touch of irony as the Detroit Pistons welcomed their Central Division rival, the Indiana Pacers. Prior to tip off, the Pistons unveiled the 2002-03 division banner, which back division titles, 100 wins and an Eastern Conference Finals berth. The Piston faithful greeted the former Coach of the Year with a standing ovation.

"That was really nice," said Carlisle, who also received a pre-game hug from Ben Wallace. "It was a classy gesture from a classy organization to do that and they didn't have to."

> "That was really nice. It was a classy gesture from a classy organization to do that and they didn't have to."

RICK CARLISLE

The former Pistons coach on receiving a standing ovation from the Detroit fans on opening night of the 2003-04 season.

was raised to the rafters while the man responsible for directing Detroit the previous season watched from the opposing team's bench. In a controversial offseason move, his successor, Larry Brown, was brought in under the directive to do something he had not, bring home an NBA championship. Yet on the night fans welcomed their 63-year-old Hall of Fame coach, they also paid homage to the man who guided the Pistons to back-to-

The Larry Brown era officially began with a loss as the Pacers squeaked by with an 89-87 victory. Brown wasn't the only newcomer to the Pistons as the team welcomed six new players and said goodbye to key bench contributors Jon Barry, Clifford Robinson and Michael Curry. Second-year players Tayshaun Prince and Mehmet Okur assumed larger roles as the Pistons headed into Philadelphia on November 26th with a 10-5 record.

RICK CARLISLE RETURNS TO THE PALACE OF AUBURN HILLS ON OPENING NIGHT.

THE SIXER FANS WELCOME LARRY BROWN IN HIS FIRST VISIT TO PHILLY AS DETROIT HEAD COACH.

The highly anticipated showdown marked the first return appearance for Brown since he had left the team he had successfully guided for six seasons, which included an NBA Finals appearance. While some passionate Philly fans expressed their displeasure in welcoming their former coach, many of Brown's former players hugged the man who played a critical role in their lives.

"The beginning of the game made it for me," said Brown. "I don't know if ever I've been more moved in a game. People that mean something to me really extended themselves. From that standpoint, it doesn't get any better than that for me. What those players did to me before the game ... it brings closure to a lot of stuff."

The New Year began as the old one left off, with the Pistons riding a consecutive game winning streak, which reached 13 going back to December 27 and tied a franchise mark. It was a special month for Brown, who not only notched his 900th career NBA victory when the Pistons defeated the Warriors on January 3, but also earned Eastern Conference Coach of the Month honors as well, marking the sixth time in his career.

"Rasheed and Ben can cover so much ground because they are so long."

LARRY BROWN

February wouldn't prove to be as kind to the Pistons in the standings department as Detroit struggled through a six-game losing streak. Once again, Ben Wallace, who asserted himself offensively — thanks to Brown — to a personal high scoring average of 9.5 points, was voted by fans once again to represent the Eastern Conference as the starting center in the 53rd annual NBA All-Star Game on February 15. Four days later, the Pistons welcomed a former All-Star when they acquired Rasheed Wallace in a three-team trade that sent Chucky Atkins, Lindsey Hunter to Boston and Zeljko Rebraca and Bob Sura to Atlanta.

Despite losing the first two games with Wallace in the starting lineup, the Pistons rolled to a 20-4 mark for the

"We just come into games focused on defense and
try to take away the other team's sweet spots."

CHAUNCEY BILLUPS

remainder of the season as the former North Carolina Tar Heel made an already good defense great as the Pistons held opponents to 70 points or less in eight games, including a record five in a row.

For the defensive minded Brown, having another intimidating shotblocker and rebounder in the post to go alongside a two-time Defensive Player of the Year, made the Pistons defense that much more menacing.

"When we didn't have Rasheed, a lot of times we got beat without Ben there, or if Ben was in the game and wasn't involved we had no shotblocking," said Brown. "People just took it right to the front of the rim. Rasheed and Ben can cover so much ground because they are so long."

As the team headed into the postseason riding a wave of unbridled confidence, the question remained: Would the record-setting defense be enough to carry the Pistons to the championship?

DETROIT PISTONS: BY THE NUMBERS

0	5	6	11	13
NUMBER OF PLAYERS ON THE DENVER NUGGETS WHO SCORED IN DOUBLE DIGITS IN DETROIT'S 97-66 VICTORY	AN NBA RECORD NUMBER OF CONSECUTIVE GAMES DETROIT'S DEFENSE HELD OPPONENTS UNDER 70 POINTS	LONGEST LOSING STREAK OF SEASON (FEBRUARY 3 – 17)	AN NBA RECORD NUMBER OF GAMES DETROIT'S DEFENSE HELD OPPONENTS UNDER 70 POINTS	LONGEST WINNING STREAK OF SEASON (DEC. 27 – JAN. 19)

20	84.3	5,000	10,000	900
20-6: PISTONS RECORD FOR THE REMAINDER OF THE SEASON SINCE ACQUIRING RASHEED WALLACE ON FEB. 19	AVERAGE PISTONS DEFENSE HELD OPPONENTS, WHICH IS A FRANCHISE AND LEAGUE LOW IN SHOT CLOCK ERA	RICHARD HAMILTON REACHED THIS MILESTONE IN POINTS ON NOV. 7; BEN WALLACE REACHED THIS MILESTONE IN REBOUNDS ON DEC. 26.	RASHEED WALLACE REACHED THIS MILESTONE IN POINTS ON MARCH 19.	LARRY BROWN EARNED HIS 900TH NBA CAREER VICTORY VERSUS GOLDEN STATE ON JAN. 3.

POSTSEASON

> "I think Detroit has been playing the best. Larry's teams have always played well at the back end, heading into the playoffs. They always have had very good defensive teams, and that's what you need going into the playoffs."
>
> TERRY PORTER Milwaukee Bucks Head Coach

MILWAUKEE BUCKS

FIRST ROUND

The championship quest began against a team no one had predicted would advance to the playoffs let alone secure the sixth seed in the Eastern Conference. But that's exactly what first-year head coach Terry Porter did, masterfully guiding the Milwaukee Bucks to 41 regular-season wins and a postseason appearance against the

Tayshaun Prince continued to rise to the occasion in the postseason when he scored a career playoff-high 24 points, 10 of which were netted in the third quarter of Game 5. The performance capped an excellent series for Prince, who averaged 17.4 points on 59 percent shooting while pulling down 7.6 rebounds.

	DETROIT 108	MILWAUKEE 92	DETROIT 95	DETROIT 109	DETROIT 91	
	MILWAUKEE 82	DETROIT 88	MILWAUKEE 85	MILWAUKEE 92	MILWAUKEE 77	
	G-1	G-2	G-3	G-4	G-5	

> ## "In this series, he was really on top of his game. He did a great job of getting out in the open and hitting shots on the perimeter, so he was definitely one of the X-factors for them."
>
> TERRY PORTER on Tayshaun Prince

surging Detroit Pistons. It was a series victory that appeared to be a foregone conclusion, especially given Detroit's regular-season success against Milwaukee, winning three out of four games. Factor in Detroit's addition of Rasheed Wallace and their 20-6 record as a result and there was certainly a renewed championship outlook in Motown.

After the Pistons crushed Milwaukee by 26 in Game 1, the Bucks bounced back to even the series before it shifted south for Games 3 and 4. The Bucks' hopes for an upset quickly dimmed as Detroit's backcourt of Chauncey Billups and Richard Hamilton combined for 38 and 46 points, respectively, as Detroit took command of the series, winning both games.

"In this series, he was really on top of his game," said Porter. "He did a great job of getting out in the open and hitting shots on the perimeter, so he was definitely one of the X-factors for them."

For Milwaukee, Detroit's defense proved too tough, holding Desmond Mason and Michael Redd, the Bucks' top two scorers, to 38 and 41 percent shooting, respectively.

"I think you have to give Detroit some credit," said Porter. "They really focused on trying to stop [Redd] and not letting him get anything easy. The guys that were on him made him work for everything he got, and we didn't do a good enough job of getting out in the open court and getting some easy opportunities."

NEW JERSEY NETS

This was the series Detroit wanted. This was the series Detroit needed. The repercussions of their four-game exit to the New Jersey Nets in last season's Eastern Conference Finals sent the Pistons reeling into an off-season filled with change. A new coach along with six new players plus the mid-season addition of Rasheed Wallace still didn't answer the question: Are the Pistons good

them to wins in Games 3 and 4.

It was now a best two out of three series and Game 5 turned out to be a classic, triple-overtime thriller that was filled with dramatic shots (Chauncey Billups' 40-footer to send the game into overtime) and unlikely heroes (Brian Scalabrine's 17-point performance) as Detroit fell, 127-120 before a dejected sold-out crowd at The Palace.

DETROIT 78	DETROIT 95	NEW JERSEY 82	NEW JERSEY 94	NEW JERSEY 127	DETROIT 81	DETROIT 90
NEW JERSEY 56	NEW JERSEY 80	DETROIT 64	DETROIT 79	DETROIT 120	NEW JERSEY 75	NEW JERSEY 69
G-1	G-2	G-3	G-4	G-5	G-6	G-6

> ## "We're going to enjoy this for a little while, but we really want to take that next step and try to get to the [NBA] Finals."
>
> BEN WALLACE

enough to unseat the two-time Eastern Conference Champion Nets? They would soon find out.

The Pistons immediately set the tone, overwhelming the Nets with their stifling defense, holding them to 56 points, the second-lowest point total in NBA playoff history. The Pistons continued to dominate in Game 2, winning 95-80, sending the Nets back to East Rutherford down 0-2.

Suddenly, the question became, can the Nets avoid being swept?

New Jersey, which had won 14 consecutive Eastern Conference playoff games dating back to last season, wasn't going to give up the Eastern Conference mantle so easily, especially not in New Jersey, as they bounced back, thanks to Richard Jefferson and Jason Kidd, who lifted

After going up 2-0, the Pistons were now on the verge of a major collapse having lost three straight as the series shifted back to New Jersey. If the Pistons were distressed at the possibility of being eliminated, they sure didn't show it.

"Someone said, 'You guys are loose,'" said Richard Hamilton who scored 24 points in Game 6 to lead Detroit to a 81-75 victory to force a decisive seventh game. "We've been loose all year. No reason not to be loose now."

The backcourt tandem of Billups and Hamilton made sure Detroit advanced, combining for 43 points as the Pistons pulled away in the third quarter and never looked back, winning Game 7, 90-69, as the Pistons defense held Kidd scoreless on 0-8 shooting. With last season's sweep a distant memory, the Pistons were now one round away from advancing to the NBA Finals.

INDIANA PACERS

EASTERN CONFERENCE FINALS

It was a highly anticipated match up, one that featured the top two teams in the Eastern Conference vying for the golden opportunity of advancing to the NBA Finals. It was a series overflowing with storylines — from two coaches (Larry Brown and Rick Carlisle) facing their former teams, the league's premiere defenders (Ben Wallace and Ron Artest) on opposite ends, to a legendary, clutch-

Rasheed Wallace. "You can quote me on the front page, on the back page, anywhere you want. They will not win Game 2."

Detroit backed up Wallace's bold statement, especially teammate Tayshaun Prince, whose spectacular block of a Miller breakaway layup with 17 seconds remaining in regulation not only sent the second-year player flying into the

	INDIANA 78	DETROIT 72	DETROIT 85	INDIANA 83	DETROIT 83	DETROIT 69	
	DETROIT 74	INDIANA 67	INDIANA 78	DETROIT 68	INDIANA 65	INDIANA 65	
	G-1	G-2	G-3	G-4	G-5	G-6	

"I saw him in my rear-view mirror. In hindsight, I probably should have dunked the ball, but I thought I had a few steps on him."

REGGIE MILLER on Tayshaun Prince's Game 2 block

shooting, man-in-motion guard (Reggie Miller) and his heir apparent (Richard Hamilton).

The Pacers jumped out to a 1-0 series lead thanks to Miller's late-game heroics. One of the all-time great shooters in NBA Playoff history added yet another breathless highlight to his bulging reel of dramatic shots when he nailed a three-pointer with 31 seconds left in regulation to propel Indy to a 78-74 victory.

"We've all seen it," said Pistons coach Larry Brown, who coached Miller for four seasons in Indy. "He's the best I've ever seen."

The loss placed the pressure on the Pistons to win Game 2 to avoid the daunting challenge of going down 0-2 before the series shifted to Detroit.

"They will not win Game 2," said Pistons' forward

stands but preserved Detroit's lead and ultimate victory.

"Most guys wouldn't even have ran down there," said the Pacers' Jermaine O'Neal. "He almost killed himself to block the shot."

The teams split the next two games as Hamilton and Austin Croshere starred for the Pistons and Pacers, respectively. Games 5 and 6 belonged to Hamilton and the Pistons. The player who Miller himself called "Mini-me" for his ability to move swiftly without the ball and hit clutch shots, scored a combined 55 points in both games as the Pistons advanced to the Finals for the first time since 1990.

"It's crazy," said Rip, who scored 20 or more points in eight straight games. "It still hasn't sunk in yet. It's unbelievable ... being able to play for a world title is crazy."

2004 NBA CHAMPIONS DETROIT PISTONS

59

THE FINALS

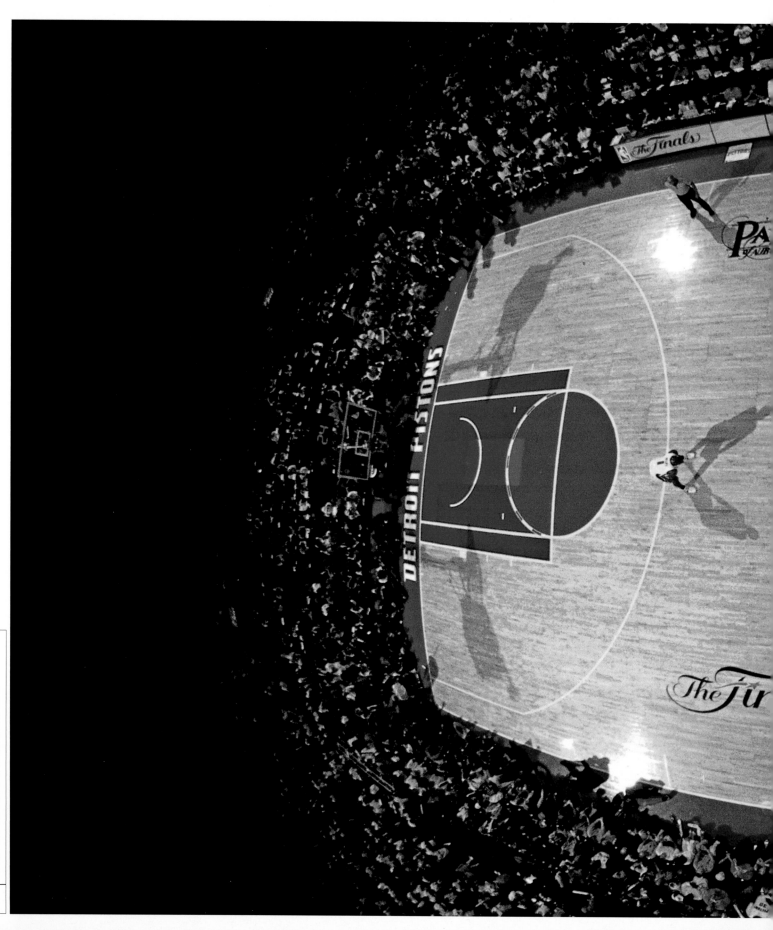

> "We have tremendous respect for the Lakers. They came out of the West and everyone knows how strong that conference is. I think they are playing at the highest level right now, so it's going to be an unbelievable challenge."

LARRY BROWN

GAME ONE

PISTONS 87

LAKERS 75

Moments before opening tip, three members of one of the greatest dynasties in NBA history approached center court as the crowd buzzed in anticipation. They are more than familiar faces to these Lakers fans. They're icons, men who comprised one of the greatest juggernauts in NBA history, combining to lead the Lakers to five titles and eight Finals appearances in the '80s. Yet Kareem Abdul-Jabbar, Magic Johnson and James Worthy of the Showtime Lakers were not only on hand for the ceremonial

NBA Finals history. The two teams clashed in the 1988 and '89 Finals, each winning a championship and although the players are now different, some things haven't changed. The Pistons muscled their way to their first Finals appearance the same way they did 15 years ago, with a relentless-stifling defense. Unlike the Pistons of the late '80s, this season's version found themselves as major underdogs against a Lakers team that won nine straight home playoff games, boasted two

"We love it that nobody expects us to win, that us-against-the world attitude. We've had it all year. You don't get to this point and not be hungry. [Malone and Payton] aren't the only ones that haven't won championships. A lot of people here haven't done it either. We want it."

RICHARD HAMILTON

honors but to also pay homage to the current Lakers dynasty, a team on the brink of accomplishing something their esteemed predecessors had not — four championships in five seasons. Four victories now separated the 21st Century Lakers from joining the short list of NBA powerhouses who accomplished such a rare feat — the Minneapolis Lakers of the '50s and the Boston Celtics of the '60s.

Game 1 of the 2004 Finals marked the third meeting between the Lakers and the Detroit Pistons in

of the league's premier players — Shaquille O'Neal and Kobe Bryant — two future Hall of Famers — Karl Malone and Gary Payton — who sacrificed salary, ego and reduced roles to be part of something special and a coach — Phil Jackson — who was on cusp of securing his league record 10th championship. Throw in the mix the Lakers' decisive edge in Finals experience — 100 games to the Pistons nine — the fact that Detroit hadn't won in Los Angeles since 1997 and the widely held belief that the Western Conference is simply the superior conference, producing

"We played Shaq and Kobe honest. They got their numbers and we played everybody else honest. We didn't let the role players come out and just line up shots from the outside."

BEN WALLACE

> # "People underestimate Tayshaun. He's 6-9, but when he stretches out, he's seven feet. Kobe is probably the best one-on-one player in the game, so you have to contest his shots. Tayshaun did a great job staying with him."

CHAUNCEY BILLUPS on teammate Tayshaun Prince's defense of Kobe Bryant

the last five NBA champions and it's little wonder why the Pistons even bothered to show up for the 58th annual Finals.

Unfazed and undaunted by the global championship center stage in which more than 200 countries and an audience of approximately 3.1 billion people through NBA Entertainment's television, film and digital technology tuned in, the Pistons wanted to write championship history of their own on the anniversary date of their Game 1 victory over the Lakers in Los Angeles in 1989. Detroit took a major step in securing the franchise's third title in 16 years by employing a strategy few teams have had success in implementing, single coverage of O'Neal. The three-time Finals MVP took full advantage, scoring the Lakers' first 10 points on his way to a 20-point first half as L.A. clinged to a 41-40 lead.

The second half saw the Pistons jump out to an eight-point lead thanks in part to Chauncey Billups

whose combination of jumpers and drives to the hoop netted him 20 points at the end of three quarters as Detroit outscored the Lakers 24-17. While O'Neal was successful in scoring against the Pistons' man-to-man defense, the rest of the Lakers struggled. Kobe Bryant had 6-9 small forward Tayshaun Prince draped all over him throughout the game and needed 27 shots to finish with 25 points.

> # "I wanted to set the tone. I am a shooter, man. I can score."

CHAUNCEY BILLUPS

The 6-3 guard averaged 26.5 points versus the Lakers during the regular season. Billups scored 11 points in the first quarter en route to a team high 22.

"They wanted it a little more than we did. We were lackadaisical."

SHAQUILLE O'NEAL

The Pistons thwarted any hope of a Lakers comeback in the fourth quarter as the Pistons took turns delivering clutch baskets whether it was Prince, Billups or Rasheed Wallace as they built a 13-point lead. When the final buzzer sounded, the Pistons had accomplished what few people outside of Detroit, Michigan thought was possible; defeat the heavily favored Lakers on their home floor while holding the NBA's third highest scoring team, who averaged 98 points throughout the season, to 75 points.

While O'Neal and Bryant combined for 59 of the team's 75 points, the Lakers reserves accounted for only 16 points on 6-for-30 shooting.

"I don't know if we could ever defend better," said Pistons coach Larry Brown, who also led the Philadelphia 76ers to a Game 1 upset in the Finals in Los Angeles three years earlier. "We contested shots. We did an unbelievable job, and that's what it's going to take."

PISTONS

PLAYER	POS	MIN	FGM-A	3PM-A	FTM-A	OFF	DEF	TOT	AST	PF	ST	TO	BS	PTS
R. HAMILTON	G	43	5-16	0-0	2-4	3	4	7	5	0	1	6	0	12
C. BILLUPS	G	39	8-14	2-4	4-4	1	2	3	4	1	3	2	0	22
T. PRINCE	F	35	5-10	1-4	0-0	1	5	6	4	3	2	0	0	11
R. WALLACE	F	29	3-4	2-2	6-6	1	7	8	1	3	0	1	1	14
B. WALLACE	C	41	4-8	0-0	1-2	1	7	8	0	1	1	2	1	9
E. CAMPBELL		18	2-5	0-0	2-6	1	0	1	4	1	2	1	2	6
L. HUNTER		13	1-5	1-2	2-2	0	1	1	0	2	0	1	0	5
C. WILLIAMSON		11	2-3	0-0	3-4	1	1	2	1	3	0	0	0	7
M. OKUR		6	0-0	0-0	1-2	0	0	0	0	1	0	1	0	1
D. HAM		4	0-0	0-0	0-0	0	0	0	0	2	0	0	0	0
M. JAMES		1	0-0	0-0	0-0	0	0	0	0	0	0	0	0	0
D. MILICIC														
TOTAL		240	30-65	6-12	21-30	9	27	36	19	17	9	14	4	87

LOS ANGELES LAKERS

PLAYER	POS	MIN	FGM-A	3PM-A	FTM-A	OFF	DEF	TOT	AST	PF	ST	TO	BS	PTS
K. BRYANT	G	47	10-27	1-6	4-4	1	3	4	4	2	4	3	2	25
G. PAYTON	G	31	1-4	1-1	0-0	1	1	2	3	5	2	2	0	3
K. MALONE	F	44	2-9	0-0	0-0	3	8	11	3	1	0	0	1	4
D. GEORGE	F	27	2-5	1-2	0-0	0	3	3	0	2	1	1	0	5
S. O'NEAL	C	45	13-16	0-0	8-12	5	6	11	1	4	0	6	1	34
D. FISHER		20	1-9	0-2	0-0	3	0	3	3	2	1	1	0	2
K. RUSH		16	0-3	0-2	0-0	0	2	2	0	4	0	2	0	0
S. MEDVEDENKO		6	0-0	0-0	2-2	0	1	1	0	3	0	0	0	2
R. FOX		4	0-0	0-0	0-0	0	0	0	1	2	0	0	0	0
B. COOK														
L. WALTON														
B. RUSSELL														
TOTAL		240	29-73	3-13	14-18	13	24	37	15	25	8	15	4	75

2004 NBA CHAMPIONS DETROIT PISTONS

69

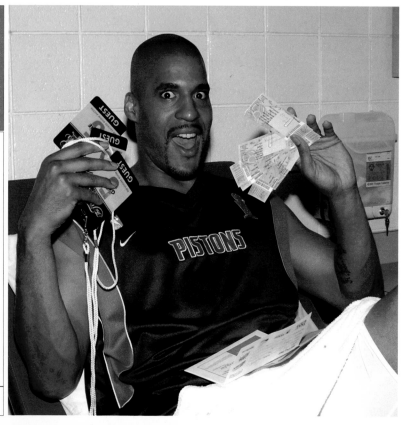

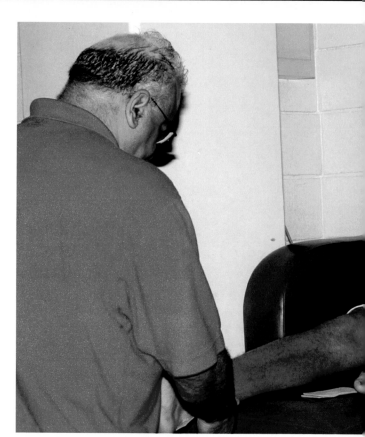

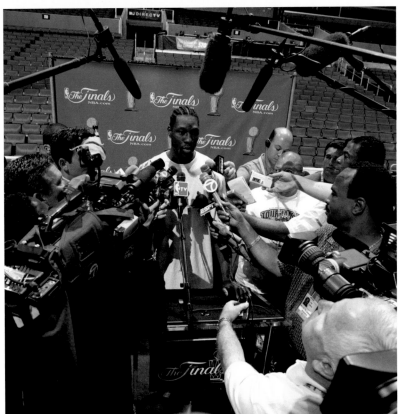

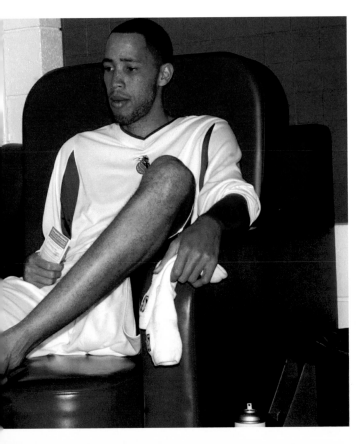

GAME TWO

PISTONS 91

LAKERS 99 OT

In a mere matter of 48 hours, the mood in Southern California had shifted dramatically as the heavily favored Lakers were now confronted with a 0-1 series deficit. Suddenly, the boundless optimisim and dreams of championship parades along Figueroa Boulevard that ran rampant before Sunday's game were now replaced with a nervous sense of anticipation at Staples Center as the sell-out crowd, many of whom had worn their heroes' numbers on their backs, had

"I went on the back of the bus after Game 1 and told them, you know, we had won a tough Game 1 [with the 76ers] and then kind of felt pretty proud of ourselves and then lo and behold, Phil [Jackson] got them ready, they won four straight," said Brown.

"And they all looked at me and said, we're not the same team.

"I said, 'Well, that's not what I'm worried about. You've got the same coach.'"

> ## "They know this is going to be a dogfight. We woke them up. This is going to be a long series, and they know we are in it."
>
> CHAUNCEY BILLUPS

eagerly settled into their seats. This feeling of anxiousness isn't anything new to the Laker faithful as the team found itself in a similar position three years ago when the Philadelphia 76ers upset the heavily favored Lakers in overtime of Game 1 of the Finals. The man calling the shots for the underdog Sixers that year understood the golden opportunity presented before his team shortly before Game 2 was set to tip off.

It appeared in the early going that Brown and the Pistons would not suffer the same fate as his former team as the Pistons quickly dispelled any thoughts of a Game 1 fluke win, flawlessly executing plays with precision while the Lakers turned the ball over with regularity to the tune of six in the first quarter. This was not the start the Lakers fans had envisioned as the murmur in the crowd grew louder. They knew that no team in Finals history had ever come back from an 0-2 deficit to win the championship.

Trailing 11-10 and in desperate need of an infusion of positive energy, Phil Jackson looked to his bench — a supporting cast that had under delivered in Game 1 with a four-point effort — and inserted the first sub into the game with 3:30 remaining in the first quarter. Racing down the Lakers sideline was Luke Walton, a promising rookie out of the University of Arizona, who had averaged 4.4 minutes in 13 playoff appearances up to that point. It was somewhat of a curious move by Jackson given the fact that the son of Hall of Famer Bill Walton had posted back-to-back DNPs in the two previous playoff games. Yet, Jackson, as he has done all season, called the right number as the 24-year-old small forward re-energized his team and the Staples Center

> ### "Luke Walton was phenomenal. He came into the game and gave them a huge lift."
>
> LARRY BROWN

crowd with a dazzling all-around display. Tapping into his playmaking abilities, Walton was everywhere, moving the ball, draining rainbow jumpers, going coast to coast, finishing in transition and diving for loose balls. He was the Lakers' new emotional leader. Soon, 18,997 strong bellowed in unison — *Luuuuuuuke* — after every one of his clutch plays as the Lakers took a 44-36 lead into halftime.

The deficit grew to 11 for the Pistons in the third quarter but thanks to the hot shooting of Chauncey Billups, who tallied 16 points in the period, Detroit zeroed in, 68-66 and the Laker faithful were getting nervous once again. The Pistons seized control in the fourth quarter with Shaquille O'Neal on the bench and when he returned, the Diesel found the Lakers trailing 89-83 with 47.8 seconds remaining. Kobe Bryant missed a three-pointer only to have O'Neal rebound and score on the missed attempt while getting fouled. After hitting the crucial free throw, which cut the lead to three, the Pistons' next possession saw Billups miss an off-balanced nine-footer as the Lakers rebounded and called a time out with 10.9 seconds remaining.

> ## "We always believe that Kobe can make miracle shots, even when things are not going well for him. That was a great shot."
>
> PHIL JACKSON

Now on the brink of going down 0-2 and with the Dynasty at stake, the Lakers were in dire need of some last-second heroics and who better to deliver than the player who has compiled an impressive video package of buzzer-beaters and clutch baskets in his young career.

With every one of the nearly 19,000 fans on their feet and virtually breathless in anticipation, Karl Malone inbounded the ball to O'Neal who passed it to Walton who then swung it to Bryant. Located on the left wing, Bryant went to work on his defender, Richard Hamilton, a former prep high school rival from their high school days in the Philadelphia area. As the clock wound down, Bryant dribbled as he stared down Hamilton who threw his arms up in the air but couldn't prevent the 28-foot attempt from sailing over his head on its way to tying the game with 2.1 seconds remaining. The Staples Center erupted as Bryant made arguably the biggest shot in the Lakers' rich history to save their season. The game went

> ## "We defended it. We switched. A great player made a great shot ... We don't foul in a situation like that. He's going to go up and shoot it any way."
>
> LARRY BROWN

into overtime as the Lakers rode the wave of momentum, overwhelming the Pistons, 10-2, as Bryant contributed eight points, to even the series.

While Bryant grabbed the heroic headlines, which were splashed all over the world that night and the next day, it was the brilliant play of the rookie who really saved the day for the Lakers.

"You can talk about my shot all night long," Bryant said after the game. "But without Luke in the game playing as well as he did, we wouldn't be in that position."

"We had them on the ropes. There's no ifs, ands or buts.
We had them on the ropes and they got out."

CHAUNCEY BILLUPS

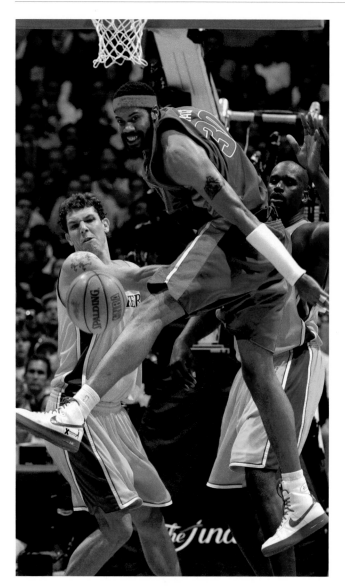

PISTONS

PLAYER	POS	MIN	FGM-A	3PM-A	FTM-A	OFF	DEF	TOT	AST	PF	ST	TO	BS	PTS
R. HAMILTON	G	47	10-25	2-2	4-5	5	3	8	2	2	0	5	0	26
C. BILLUPS	G	47	6-15	2-2	13-14	2	2	4	9	1	0	3	0	27
T. PRINCE	F	47	2-6	1-2	0-0	4	1	5	0	2	3	0	2	5
R. WALLACE	F	34	5-14	0-3	1-2	1	6	7	3	4	0	0	2	11
B. WALLACE	C	43	5-11	0-0	2-8	4	10	14	1	5	2	0	2	12
M. OKUR		18	0-2	0-0	1-2	0	2	2	1	2	0	3	0	1
L. HUNTER		12	2-4	1-3	0-0	0	0	0	2	1	1	0	0	5
E. CAMPBELL		9	1-2	0-0	0-0	2	2	4	1	4	0	1	0	2
C. WILLIAMSON		7	1-2	0-0	0-0	1	1	2	0	2	0	2	0	2
M. JAMES		1	0-0	0-0	0-0	0	0	0	0	0	0	0	0	0
D. HAM	DNP													
D. MILICIC	DNP													
TOTAL		265	32-81	6-12	21-31	19	27	46	19	23	6	14	6	91

LOS ANGELES LAKERS

PLAYER	POS	MIN	FGM-A	3PM-A	FTM-A	OFF	DEF	TOT	AST	PF	ST	TO	BS	PTS
K. BRYANT	G	49	14-27	1-5	4-5	0	4	4	7	5	2	5	0	33
G. PAYTON	G	28	1-3	0-1	0-0	1	2	3	3	4	1	3	0	2
K. MALONE	F	39	3-9	0-1	3-4	3	6	9	2	3	1	1	0	9
D. GEORGE	F	21	3-7	1-3	0-0	0	2	2	1	2	1	0	0	7
S. O'NEAL	C	48	10-20	0-0	9-14	3	4	7	3	5	0	3	1	29
L. WALTON		27	3-3	1-1	0-0	1	4	5	8	3	0	0	2	7
D. FISHER		25	2-6	2-4	1-2	0	3	3	2	4	2	0	0	7
K. RUSH		18	2-4	1-2	0-0	0	2	2	2	0	0	1	0	5
S. MEDVEDENKO		9	0-1	0-0	0-0	1	2	3	0	1	0	0	0	0
B. COOK		1	0-0	0-0	0-0	0	0	0	0	0	0	1	0	0
R. FOX	DNP													
B. RUSSELL	DNP													
TOTAL		265	38-80	6-17	17-25	9	29	38	28	27	7	14	3	99

GAME THREE

LAKERS 68

| G-1 | G-2 | G-3 | G-4 | G-5 |

PISTONS 88

How would the Pistons respond following Game 2's heartbreaking loss? What kind of lingering effects would Kobe Bryant's stunning three-pointer have on a team many thought should be up 2-0? Was it sound strategy for the Pistons not to foul Shaquille O'Neal or any of the other Lakers, most notably Bryant, with the clock winding down to play them honest for the final 10.9 seconds of regulation? As the Pistons prepared to host their first Finals home game in 14 years, Larry Brown and his players

signs dotted this world-reknowned facility that inspired a wave of new arenas after it was constructed in 1988. ThunderStix cracked in unison at every opportunity as special flame shooters burst above the baskets during the Piston pre-game player introductions while P.A. announcer John Mason stoked the crowd as decibel levels hit a fever pitch:

B-b-b-b-b-b-b-b-b-en W-w-w-w-w-w-w-allace ...
Feeding off their high-energy fans, the Pistons raced

"Larry Brown teams always bounce back. They fight hard and they play hard."

KOBE BRYANT

---

pondered these questions and more in what must have been the longest four-plus hour flight from Los Angeles to Detroit. No one felt the brunt of the criticism more than Brown who made the choice not to foul Bryant to avoid the risk of a four-point play or at the very least three foul shots. In 21 years as an NBA head coach, the Hall of Famer never had to endure such a stream of second guessing from print and broadcast journalists from all over the world as he did for the next 44 hours until Game 3 tipped off.

It didn't take the Pistons long to answer the myriad of questions that hovered over them as The Palace of Auburn Hills served as the perfect tonic for any type of Game 2 hangover that the players may have experienced as 22,076 raucous fans welcomed their basketball heroes home. A sea of blue and white No. 3 and 30 jerseys, painted red, white and blue faces, Ben Wallace afro-style wigs worn by all ages along with countless homemade

out to an 8-0 lead, applying a relentless full-court pressure to their visitors from the West Coast. Richard Hamilton, who was on the defensive end of Kobe Bryant's three-point masterpiece in Game 2, was a man on a mission. The 6-6 guard was in perpetual motion, moving fluidly without the ball, then draining jumpers and bank shots on his way to eight first-quarter points while his high school rival — Bryant — went scoreless as he attempted only three field goals. Chauncey Billups who starred in the first two games of the series, was equally effective as he and his backcourtmate combined for 22 points in the first half, outplaying the Lakers' counterpart tandem of Bryant and Gary Payton who only managed one point between them. Although L.A.'s offensive output was within two points of tying the lowest scoring half of a Finals game in the shot-clock era, thanks to Shaquille O'Neal's inside dominance, which resulted in 12 points, the Lakers were still within seven at halftime, trailing 39-32.

"They beat us to every loose ball."

SHAQUILLE O'NEAL

The third quarter wasn't much better as the Lakers couldn't match Detroit's high energy and crisp ball movement while their defensive rotation was a step too slow in reacting to this balanced offense. As they have done for the first two games, the Pistons dominated the third quarter, outscoring the Lakers 24-19. Everyone contributed. Whether it was Elden Campbell stealing the ball and finishing on a fastbreak dunk, Lindsey Hunter blocking shots and grabbing rebounds or Corliss Williamson providing some scoring punch off the bench, the train whistle on The Palace's video board was working overtime, denoting the number of hustle plays. The Pistons eventually ran up a 20-point lead early in the

"For the most part, tonight I was attacking 30 feet from the basket."

KOBE BRYANT

fourth quarter and cruised as O'Neal was limited to only three shots in the second half while his teammate Karl Malone struggled with a sprained right knee, scoring only five points in 18 minutes of action. With 1:48 remaining, the Pistons' rookie and fan favorite Darko Milicic entered the game as the route was near complete. When the smoke cleared inside The Palace, the Pistons defense held the Lakers to 68 points, their third lowest offensive output in Finals history in the 50 years of the shot clock's existence.

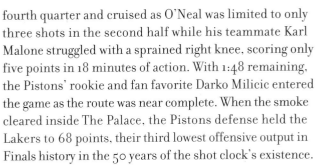

Shaquille O'Neal, who historically has made the Finals his personal showcase, was limited to an all-time championship series low of 14 points. In 21 career Finals games, the three-time Finals MVP had never been below the 25-point mark. Bryant, who had averaged 29 points in the first two games, couldn't shake loose from Tayshaun Prince, and scored only 11 points on 4 for 13 shooting.

"You can't guard better than Tayshaun guarded."

LARRY BROWN

Tayshaun Prince limited Kobe Bryant to a Finals low of 11 points on 4 for 13 shooting.

The O'Neal-Bryant tandem, which had averaged 60.5 points in the series, were held to 25 on a night the Pistons seized control of the series.

"I don't think we can defend better than tonight," said Brown, who made a similar statement after Detroit's Game 1 win, but soon corrected himself after watching his team force the Lakers into 16 turnovers and limit them to 36.5% shooting.

Forty eight hours had passed since the Pistons' lonesome night in Los Angeles as the fortunes of the series had now changed dramatically. When Brown was asked after the game how he anticipated the Lakers would respond in Game 4, the Hall of Famer replied:

"I don't even want to think about that. God, you guys – I almost committed suicide on the flight back from L.A. I'm going to enjoy this."

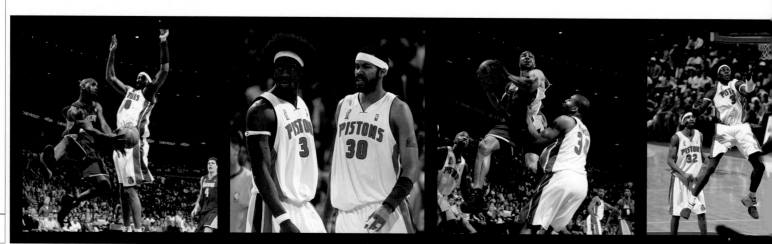

"You know, we're faced with a heckuva challenge right now, being down 2-1 and to have two games coming up on their home floor. This is a good crowd and they feed off that."

KOBE BRYANT

LOS ANGELES LAKERS

PLAYER	POS	MIN	FGM-A	3PM-A	FTM-A	OFF	DEF	TOT	AST	PF	ST	TO	BS	PTS
K. BRYANT	G	45	4-13	0-4	3-3	0	3	3	5	3	1	4	1	11
G. PAYTON	G	35	2-7	1-5	1-2	1	3	4	7	2	1	0	1	6
K. MALONE	F	18	2-4	0-0	1-2	0	4	4	2	2	0	1	0	8
D. GEORGE	F	21	3-8	2-6	0-0	0	3	3	0	3	2	1	1	5
S. O'NEAL	C	38	7-14	0-0	0-2	2	6	8	1	5	1	2	0	14
S. MEDVEDENKO		21	1-3	0-0	1-2	2	6	8	1	4	0	1	1	3
L. WALTON		19	1-5	0-2	2-2	1	2	3	2	4	1	2	0	4
K. RUSH		18	3-8	2-7	0-0	0	1	1	0	2	1	2	0	8
D. FISHER		16	4-9	1-3	0-0	1	1	2	1	1	0	3	0	9
B. COOK		8	0-3	0-0	0-0	0	3	3	0	2	0	0	0	0
B. RUSSELL		1	0-0	0-0	0-0	0	0	0	0	0	0	0	0	0
R. FOX	DNP													
TOTAL		240	27-74	6-27	8-13	7	32	39	19	28	7	16	4	68

PISTONS

PLAYER	POS	MIN	FGM-A	3PM-A	FTM-A	OFF	DEF	TOT	AST	PF	ST	TO	BS	PTS
R. HAMILTON	G	43	11-22	2-4	7-7	3	3	6	3	1	2	3	0	31
C. BILLUPS	G	36	5-11	2-5	7-7	0	2	2	3	1	1	2	0	19
T. PRINCE	F	36	5-13	1-5	0-2	3	3	6	2	1	0	1	0	11
R. WALLACE	F	26	1-4	0-0	1-4	2	8	10	1	3	0	1	2	3
B. WALLACE	C	38	3-9	0-1	1-4	2	9	11	3	3	2	3	0	7
L. HUNTER		16	1-3	0-0	0-0	1	4	5	2	4	0	0	2	2
C. WILLIAMSON		15	2-4	0-0	2-2	0	3	3	0	0	3	1	0	6
E. CAMPBELL		13	1-4	0-0	3-4	2	0	2	1	3	0	0	0	5
M. OKUR		8	1-4	0-0	0-0	1	3	4	1	0	0	0	0	2
M. JAMES		4	0-0	0-0	0-0	1	0	1	1	0	0	0	0	0
D. HAM		3	1-1	0-0	0-0	0	0	0	0	0	0	0	0	2
D. MILICIC		2	0-1	0-0	0-0	0	1	1	0	0	0	0	0	0
TOTAL		240	31-76	5-15	21-30	15	36	51	17	16	11	11	4	88

GAME FOUR

LAKERS 80

PISTONS 88

| G-1 | G-2 | G-3 | G-4 | G-5 |

In less than one week the Los Angeles Lakers went from prohibitive favorites to a team that was reeling, desperately searching for answers after being overwhelmed in Game 3 by a younger, longer, hungrier and more athletic Pistons team that was now surging towards its first NBA championship in 14 years. The balance of the series had experienced a major shift and Phil Jackson and his coaching staff had two days to chart a new course in order to assure a return trip

input? It was an interesting dilemma for the nine-time NBA championship coach who was staring at a 2-1 series deficit for the first time in his Finals experience. The rain soaked days in Eastern Michigan between games gave both teams plenty of time indoors to fine tune their adjustments in what amounted to be a must-win game for the Lakers.

Moments after Detroit native Kid Rock sang "America The Beautiful," and despite a hint during his pre-game press conference that a change may be in store, Jackson

"We thought this was the biggest game of the series. We said this is no time to celebrate. This team has been here before."

CHAUNCEY BILLUPS

to Los Angeles for Game 6. What path would they choose? Would Karl Malone, who had valiantly played in this series despite harboring a badly damaged right knee, be able to square up against the younger, quicker Rasheed Wallace? Would Jackson send another veteran, Gary Payton, to the bench given his difficulties guarding the quicker Chauncey Billups who had badly outplayed the nine-time All-Star and former Defensive Player of the Year to the scoring advantage tune of 68-11? Sensing the urgency, even the Lakers championship core of Shaquille O'Neal, Kobe Bryant, Derek Fisher, Rick Fox and Devean George cornered their coach in the men's room at The Palace on one of the off days to strongly encourage a lineup change to help improve the team's uneven offensive execution, which had struggled mightily against Detroit's ultra-quick, suffocating defense. Would Jackson heed their

opted to return to the same starting lineup; but it wasn't long before he needed to make a switch. Devean George picked up two fouls in the game's first 90 seconds and quickly off the bench came Fox, who missed 44 games during the regular season as a result of offseason surgery on his left foot. The veteran contributed immediately, chipping in with three assists on the Lakers first four baskets while also scoring in the post. The Lakers' game plan was to force feed Shaquille O'Neal and it was an effective strategy at that as he feasted on single defensive coverage, amassing 13 points and seven rebounds in the first 15 minutes of action. While O'Neal was keeping the Lakers in the game, racking up first-half numbers of 17 and 12, Bryant continued his struggles from the field, connecting on only three baskets out of 14 attempts as the Lakers trailed 41-39 going into halftime.

"Give credit to the Pistons. They handled the adversity of Shaq's great game and kept their composure and found a way to get to the foul line."

PHIL JACKSON

While the Lakers outscored the Pistons 17-15 in the third quarter to draw even at 56 heading into the fourth, the next 12 minutes would leave an indelible impression on not only the game but the series. The underdog Pistons seized control with an assortment of players taking their collective swipe at the Lakers dynasty. First, Richard Hamilton scored the first four points of the fourth quarter and then at the 6:26 mark, Chauncey Billups nailed the first of two big three-pointers as Detroit increased its lead, 70-64. Rasheed Wallace, who had been mired in foul trouble throughout the series, picked the perfect time to enjoy his best game of the Finals, converting on four of six field goals and routinely answering the Lakers' comeback attempts. Alley-oop jam, fadeaway, mid-range jumpers, clutch free throws, Wallace was showing his expansive offensive game as fans shouted "Sheeeeeeed" on each of his possessions. The Lakers couldn't stop Wallace as Karl Malone sat helplessly on the bench saddled with his injured knee after being removed at the four-in-a-half minute mark in the third quarter.

"I knew Karl was a little hobbled, so that was one of the weaknesses in their defense," said Wallace, who rebounded from a three-point first half and ended up with 26 points and 13 rebounds for the game. "That's something we had to attack. He has a bad knee or whatever, so we can't have no sympathy for that."

O'Neal, who was unstoppable throughout the game, tallying 36 points and 20 rebounds, barely saw the ball

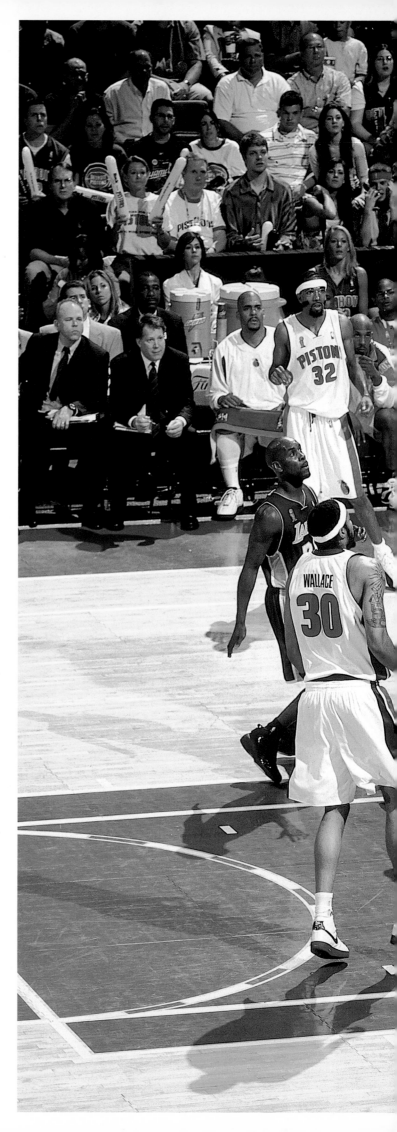

"Some of them were good and some of them stunk. That's pretty much every game with me."

KOBE BRYANT

The All-Star shooting guard finished with 20 points on 8 of 25 shooting, 2 assists, 0 rebounds and 2 free throw attempts in 45 minutes

down the stretch while Bryant couldn't shake Tayshaun Prince and Detroit's rotating defense, routinely misfiring on long-range field goal attempts on his way to an 8 of 25 performance. As the game was slipping away, Bryant showed his frustration for his subpar play by picking up a technical foul with five minutes remaining. Any thoughts of a Lakers comeback were quickly dashed when Wallace nailed a jumper with one minute remaining to give the Pistons a commanding 86-78 lead. The clutch basket was reflective of a sizzling quarter for the Pistons who shot 58.8 % from the field compared to the Lakers 33.3%.

"Our defense has dictated the series."

RICHARD HAMILTON

One look at the box score showed another all-around balanced game from the Pistons. In addition to Wallace's 26 points, Billups and Hamilton, who combined for 19 points in the fourth quarter, posted 23 and 17 for the game, respectively, while Ben Wallace pulled down 13 rebounds. Once again, the Pistons' energy, quickness and aggressive play resulted in another distinct advantage from the free throw line where they paraded 41 times compared to the Lakers,

who led the league in free throw attempts during the regular season, with 22.

Asked during the postgame press conference whether he was worried that his team may be overconfident since no team in NBA Finals history had lost the series being up 3-1, Pistons coach Larry Brown replied:

"I think this group can deal with it because they are trying their darndest to do it the right way. So there's no need even thinking about what no team did."

LAKERS

PLAYER	POS	MIN	FGM-A	3PM-A	FTM-A	OFF	DEF	TOT	AST	PF	ST	TO	BS	PTS
K. BRYANT	G	45	8-25	2-6	2-2	0	0	0	2	3	1	3	0	20
G. PAYTON	G	43	4-11	0-2	0-0	1	1	2	5	4	0	1	0	8
K. MALONE	F	21	1-2	0-0	0-0	2	3	5	2	2	0	2	0	2
D. GEORGE	F	15	1-2	1-2	2-4	1	2	3	0	5	1	0	0	5
S. O'NEAL	C	47	16-21	0-0	4-11	3	17	20	2	4	0	2	1	36
D. FISHER		21	1-6	0-3	2-3	1	4	5	2	4	0	0	0	4
R. FOX		16	1-4	0-1	0-0	0	1	1	6	3	0	0	0	2
S. MEDVEDENKO		13	1-5	0-0	1-2	1	0	1	1	3	0	0	0	3
L. WALTON		12	0-1	0-1	0-0	0	1	1	3	6	2	2	0	0
K. RUSH		6	0-1	0-1	0-0	0	0	0	1	0	0	0	0	0
B. RUSSELL		1	0-0	0-0	0-0	0	0	0	0	0	0	0	0	0
B. COOK	DNP													
TOTAL		240	33-78	3-16	11-22	9	29	38	23	35	4	10	1	80

PISTONS

PLAYER	POS	MIN	FGM-A	3PM-A	FTM-A	OFF	DEF	TOT	AST	PF	ST	TO	BS	PTS
R. HAMILTON	G	44	5-11	0-0	7-7	1	1	2	6	5	0	5	0	17
C. BILLUPS	G	37	7-12	2-5	7-9	0	4	4	4	3	2	3	0	23
T. PRINCE	F	40	3-10	0-3	0-1	4	3	7	2	1	0	0	0	6
R. WALLACE	F	41	10-23	0-5	6-6	2	11	13	2	4	2	2	2	26
B. WALLACE	C	39	2-5	0-0	4-14	2	11	13	2	3	1	1	1	8
E. CAMPBELL		14	0-3	0-0	0-0	0	2	2	0	2	0	0	1	0
L. HUNTER		11	0-1	0-0	4-4	0	0	0	0	1	0	0	0	4
M. JAMES		6	2-2	0-0	0-0	0	2	2	0	0	0	1	0	4
C. WILLIAMSON		5	0-1	0-0	0-0	0	2	2	0	0	0	0	0	0
D. HAM		2	0-0	0-0	0-0	0	0	0	0	1	0	0	0	0
D. MILICIC		1	0-0	0-0	0-0	0	0	0	0	0	0	0	0	0
M. OKUR	DNP													
TOTAL		240	29-68	2-13	28-41	9	36	45	16	20	5	12	4	88

GAME FIVE

LAKERS 87

| G-1 | G-2 | G-3 | G-4 | G-5 |

PISTONS 100

Taking a cue from the Black Eyed Peas hit song, "Let's get it started," which was played throughout ABC's coverage of The Finals, Detroit fans did just that, arriving four hours before tip off under beautiful blue skies in Auburn Hills, Michigan, in anticipation of celebrating the Pistons first NBA championship at home. Diehard followers started filing into the parking lot as tailgaters wore their favorite Detroit jerseys, appearing the least bit concerned that their Pistons wouldn't finish the job that began nine days ago. Television trucks dotted the area as local news

was a daunting challenge, one that would have to begin in front of 22,071 raucous fans who now dripped with anxiousness in saluting their team's first NBA title at home. Despite the insurmountable odds, Lakers coach Phil Jackson remained unfazed at the task ahead.

"We don't care about the records of teams in this situation in the past," said Jackson. "We believe that we can turn this thing around."

Yet Detroit was looking to make history of their own by becoming the first team to win the middle three games

"It's crazy. It's unbelievable, man. We believed. We didn't worry about what people wrote, what was said on TV or what was being said in Las Vegas. We said to ourselves anything is possible if we play together as five on the offensive and defensive end."

RICHARD HAMILTON

correspondents described the festive atmosphere live with up-to-the minute reports. Inside the arena, a numbing calm hovered over the Los Angeles locker room as the Lakers, winners of three of the last four NBA championships, were now a loss away from a summer of uncertainty. No team in Finals history has ever bounced back from a 3-1 series deficit and the Lakers were vying to become the first team to do so. It

since the Finals schedule went to the 2-3-2 format in 1985.

Prior to tip off, questions swirled around the status of Karl Malone and whether the NBA's second all-time leading scorer would be able to suit up due to his sprained right knee ligament. When he walked onto the court in street clothes moments before the game, it was apparent any type of Lakers comeback attempt would need a healthy boost from his replacement, Slava Medvedenko.

2004 NBA CHAMPIONS DETROIT PISTONS

With some words of encouragement from Malone, the 6-10 power forward from the Ukraine responded, making four baskets and recording an assist in the game's first six minutes as the Lakers jumped out to a 14-7 lead. The Lakers' quick start was tempered due to Shaquille O'Neal picking up two quick fouls in the first four minutes and two seconds of action. With O'Neal on the bench, the Pistons went to work, racing to an 8-0 run in the next 1:36. Detroit surged to the biggest half-time lead of the series, 55-45, thanks to the combination of Mehmet Okur and Ben Wallace who scored 13 points in the last six minutes of the second quarter as the Pistons

> ## "We just took it to 'em. We knew we could play with anybody in this league and I think we showed it."
>
> TAYSHAUN PRINCE

shot a sizzling 61 percent from the field heading into intermission. The official celebration was now only 24 minutes from commencement.

The wave of momentum continued in the second half when Rasheed Wallace nailed a three-pointer within the first 15 seconds of the third quarter as the Pistons continued to attack the boards, pulling down five offensive rebounds in the first six minutes. The lead would eventually build to 17, thanks to a tip-in slam by Wallace, who had the gong working overtime at The Palace, delivering his best all-around game of the series. The undrafted All-Star center out of Virginia Union, once again did it on both ends, not only limiting O'Neal's effectiveness with three first-half fouls but mixing it up offensively with a combination of layups, dunks and mid-range jumpers on his way to an 18-point, 22-rebound effort. The route was on as Detroit enjoyed a 23-point lead at the end of the third quarter, 82-59. When Lindsey Hunter stole the ball from Kobe Bryant to begin the fourth, it was more than apparent that Three Championship Drive was soon going to be receiving a new name. The Pistons went on to win by 13 with all five starters posting double digits in scoring while nine players scored in all.

"They do play the right way, and I'm very proud of them."

LARRY BROWN

The Pistons' victory will go down as one of the greatest upsets — if not the greatest — in NBA Finals history, yet a closer look at the numbers raises the question; 'Was it really an upset?' Is it an upset when a team defeats another team by an average of 13.3 points? Or outrebounds them and shoots 60 more free throws as a result of playing a more aggressive game? Is it an upset when a team such as the Lakers, whose offense ranked among the NBA's highest in scoring with an average of 98 points, was brought to a screeching halt with a 81.8 average? Or that only two players other than Shaquille O'Neal and Kobe Bryant posted double figures in scoring in only one game — the last one of the series?

"They played extremely well," said Lakers guard Kobe Bryant. "They coached extremely well. They executed extremely well. They played hard. They played the right way and they are deserving of the championship this year."

LAKERS

PLAYER	POS	MIN	FGM-A	3PM-A	FTM-A	OFF	DEF	TOT	AST	PF	ST	TO	BS	PTS
K. BRYANT	G	45	7-21	0-2	10-11	1	2	3	4	2	1	3	0	24
G. PAYTON	G	31	1-3	0-1	0-0	2	2	4	4	2	2	1	1	2
S. MEDVEDENKO	F	23	4-8	0-0	2-2	2	3	5	1	1	0	1	0	10
D. GEORGE	F	20	2-6	0-2	0-0	2	1	3	2	4	0	0	1	4
S. O'NEAL	C	35	7-13	0-0	6-16	2	6	8	1	4	1	1	0	20
K. RUSH		20	2-6	1-4	0-0	0	0	0	3	0	0	0	0	5
L. WALTON		19	1-4	0-2	0-0	1	3	5	2	3	3	3	0	2
D. FISHER		19	3-6	3-4	1-2	0	2	2	1	5	2	0	0	10
B. COOK		12	1-3	0-0	2-2	3	2	5	0	2	1	1	0	4
R. FOX		10	3-3	0-0	0-0	0	2	2	0	1	0	1	0	6
B. RUSSELL		6	0-2	0-1	0-0	1	0	1	0	1	0	0	0	0
K. MALONE	DNP													
TOTAL		240	31-75	4-16	21-33	14	22	36	18	27	10	11	2	87

PISTONS

PLAYER	POS	MIN	FGM-A	3PM-A	FTM-A	OFF	DEF	TOT	AST	PF	ST	TO	BS	PTS
R. HAMILTON	G	45	6-18	0-4	9-11	0	3	3	4	1	1	4	0	21
C. BILLUPS	G	33	3-5	0-1	8-8	0	3	3	6	2	0	3	0	14
T. PRINCE	F	38	6-15	0-2	5-8	3	7	10	2	2	1	1	0	17
R. WALLACE	F	21	5-8	1-2	0-0	1	0	1	0	5	0	0	1	11
B. WALLACE	C	42	8-13	0-1	2-6	10	12	22	1	3	3	0	1	18
E. CAMPBELL		14	2-2	0-0	0-0	1	3	4	2	3	0	1	0	4
C. WILLIAMSON		14	1-5	0-0	4-4	2	1	3	0	2	0	1	0	6
L. HUNTER		13	1-4	0-3	0-0	0	1	1	0	3	2	0	0	2
M. JAMES		10	0-2	0-0	0-0	1	0	1	3	2	0	0	0	0
M. OKUR		7	3-3	1-1	0-0	0	0	0	0	4	0	0	0	7
D. MILICIC		2	0-1	0-0	0-2	1	0	1	0	0	1	1	0	0
D. HAM		1	0-0	0-0	0-0	1	0	1	0	0	0	0	0	0
TOTAL		240	35-76	2-14	28-39	20	30	50	18	27	8	12	2	100

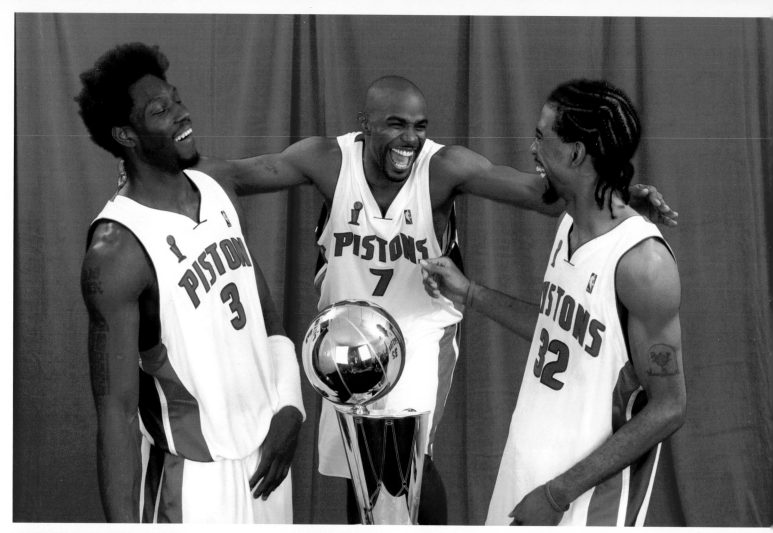

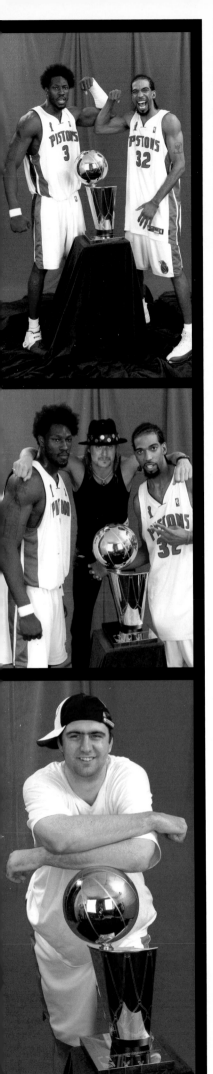

00·0

PISTONS   LAKERS
100 4 87

LDMI   PRATT & LAMBERT PAINTS   Domino's

MEIJER MEIJER www.freep.com

⬦ MANPOWER®

CHEVROLET CHEVROLET Coca-Cola